Soldier Boy

Henry George (Harry) Gilbert seen here second from left in the second-to-front row. (GILBERT FAMILY COLLECTION)

Soldier Boy

A young New Zealander
writes home from the Boer War

compiled by Kingsley Field

NH
NEW
HOLLAND

In one of the very few surviving photographs of various members of Harry Gilbert's family,
Harry's father is seen here on the right leaning on a spade, Mrs Gilbert is in the doorway, and
young Harry is thought to be the small boy dressed in a black suit standing fourth from left.
The sturdy woman in the centre of the photo was probably a maid. (GILBERT FAMILY COLLECTION)

Introduction

Somewhere, in some dim and dusty library document room, one or several little diaries may lie mouldering, uncared-for and with no one aware of their contents.

They may be the diaries of Henry George (Harry) Gilbert, a young New Zealand trooper who fought in the latter stages of the Boer War in South Africa as a member of the 7th Canterbury Mounted Rifles.

He came from the tiny rural settlement of Cust, not far from Rangiora, on the flat Canterbury Plains north-west of Christchurch in the South Island of New Zealand.

Trooper Gilbert refers to his diary several times in a series of letters he wrote home to his family during his year-long tour of duty. But, although some of those letters have survived – almost 30 have so far been discovered and transcribed – the diary (probably a series of little notebooks) appears to have vanished. These letters, however, are in themselves a truly remarkable series of documents.

Most accounts of that vicious, raw, uncensored war have come from official documents compiled by military personnel who were writing carefully weighted records. There are also newspaper reports written by journalists who were free to go where they wanted and equally as free to write whatever their imaginations fancied, and there are the writings of senior-ranked officers whose stuffed-shirt pontifications are no nearer the truth than they were to the front-line action.

Harry Gilbert's observations are different. They are told through the eyes of a 19-year-old, a youth who had spent only a few years in the "real world" of adult work and who, coming as he did from the narrow confines of a somewhat stern Anglican household in a little country village, was no doubt rather naïve.

Or was he? His letters show a quite remarkable insight into the harsh and often cruel realities of being a soldier in what was then a rigidly regimented army still under the rule of pompous British military leaders. Harry relates the hardships, the extremes of cold and heat, the thirst and hunger, the terrible brutality and often stupidity of battle, the exhilaration of hurtling across the veld on horseback straight at the enemy, the destruction of property he witnessed and took part in, and the anguish felt for the death of the British forces soldiers and the "Jackies".

Soldier Boy

For one so young he displayed a surprising sensitivity to his surroundings. At the same time he had a fortitude, resilience and pragmatism that must have carried him through times of terrible deprivation and the inevitable gut-curdling fear of battle.

During that year in South Africa, some of Harry's letters home were written on tiny scraps of paper – writing materials were always in short supply – comprising a page or two of sprawling, hurried words of reassurance to an anxious mother. Others were long and detailed, spanning several days or written during those endless, listless hours that soldiers the world over have wryly labelled the time of "hurry up and wait". These letters frequently ran to several thousand words, one of them going well over 4000, and were usually written in pencil but occasionally by the use of a dip-pen and Indian ink. It is here, in the long, rambling accounts, that young Harry Gilbert showed his astute observation and understanding, along with a vocabulary and ability to string words together that is astounding for one of his limited formal education – apparently he left school at the age of 12.

One letter, obviously written in an effort to conserve precious supplies of writing paper, was in such precise, tiny hand-writing that Harry must have sharpened his indelible pencil to a fine point at the beginning of every line. The writing is so small that in places it can be properly deciphered only with the aid of a magnifying glass.

The letters are not erudite, nor are they meant to be an overview of the battles or the politics behind the Boer War. They are simply the observations of a young man who had to rapidly come to grips with the horrible, ghastly realities of war.

By today's standards he was totally out of order in much of his choice of terminology, referring to native black South Africans and also Australian Aborigines as "niggers" and "darkies" on several occasions. But it must be remembered these letters were written more than a century ago, when such language was acceptable, at least in the circles in which Harry Gilbert lived and worked.

It should also be noted that the letters which comprise this collection have largely been transcribed as he wrote them, including errors of punctuation, and inconsistencies in his spelling and grammar, though occasionally an explanation is given where a sentence is particularly difficult to understand. The use of round brackets indicates brackets used by Harry himself in his letters; square brackets indicate an editorial explanation.

Harry's letters are documents of considerable historical significance because of their innocently honest and astutely accurate portrayal of a soldier's perspective on a war in which long-range small arms were just coming into their own. It was here, on the wide open battlefields of veld, kopje and mountain range that the then-new smokeless gunpowder was given its first serious military test, the British Tommy and the Australian and New Zealand soldiers with their Long Tom .303-inch rifles, and the Boers with their 7x57mm Mauser rifles. No longer were their firing positions given away by a telltale puff of blue smoke every time they pulled the trigger on the old black powder cartridges. And, instead of having to be within a few hundred yards with the old Snider or Martini Henry black powder rifles, the new 7mm or .303 calibres, with their high-speed, full-jacketed projectiles, could be lethal at ranges of more than 1000 yards.

It was here, too, that the young rough-and-ready Aussie and Kiwi soldiers became a problem to tradition-ridden British officers because the comparatively unsophisticated young colonials gave respect only to those who earned it, rather than to those who believed they had it as of right. Such lack of regard for status enraged the British brass – but they were more than glad to have the hardy lads from the colonies on their side when the chips were down.

Young Harry, who must have been a tough lad for all his sensitive and detailed observations, wrote what he saw, what he felt, what he heard and tasted, and also what he understood of the situations he found himself in.

Records in the Personnel Archives of the New Zealand Defence Headquarters show that Harry signed up on April 8th, 1901. This date is given on the "Attestation form for volunteers to serve with Imperial troops in South Africa" on which Harry sincerely promised and swore "that I will be faithful and bear true allegiance to His Majesty King Edward the Seventh, and that I will faithfully serve in the Volunteer Force of New Zealand both within and without the colony until I shall be lawfully discharged".

His letter home to "Dear Everybody", dated April 23rd 1901, was the first of his surviving string of mail home to various family members. That the letters have remained intact for more than a century is quite remarkable. They make extraordinary reading.

Please excuse all mistakes, blots, etc.
You cant imagine the movements
+ noise this lot has been written in

S.S. Gulf of Taranto
April 23rd 1901

Dear Everybody.

I am going to start another letter to you now that
we are once more on the briny. I must try as far as possible to start where
left off & that was in Albany. Well we had a very shiny time there &
I may as well start where we all started then, namely the beginning. The
day leave I was talking about in my last did not come off though the boat
stayed there very nearly two days. It was arranged that each man should
have four hours leave ashore & the Auckland & Wellington companies went
on the Friday afternoon leaving Canterbury to go on Saturday morning. I was
on guard from Thursday to Friday night so I was up when the steamer got
into Albany & could not have gone ashore in the afternoon even if Canterbury
had have got leave. Albany looked very nice from the steamer on Friday morning when the sun rose. It is something like Fy Heton to look at but the
hills are nothing near as high & the place is not nearly so big but as it
is built on a slope it shows up very well from the harbour. The entrance
is a good length & as it bends about a good deal you can see no sign
of the town until you get fairly into the port, when you see the town
round a bend on your right. Nothing of any importance happened on
Friday those companies went away in the launch & the others except
the ships guard, which included me, had to scrub decks & clean
rifles, but we were all eagerly looking forward to the morrow when our
turn was to come to walk land once more. Well Saturday turned
out a lovely day & at 5.30 No. 3 troop deck (ours) was the scene of some
very quick movements in the way of getting down hammocks & rolling
blankets. As everything had to be cleaned up before breakfast & all the
lower deck brushed & scrubbed you can guess that we had to be pretty

SS Gulf of Taranto
April 23ʳᵈ 1901

Please excuse all mistakes, blots, etc. You can't imagine the movements & noise this lot has been written in.

Dear Everybody

I am going to start another letter to you now that we are once more on the briny. I must try as far as possible to start where I left off, and that was in Albany. Well, we had a very shiny time there, but I may as well start where we all started then, namely the beginning.

The two days leave I was talking about in my last [letter] did not come off, though the boat stayed there very nearly two days. It was arranged that each man should have four hours leave ashore, and the Auckland and Wellington companies went on the Friday afternoon, leaving Canterbury to go on Saturday morning. I was on guard from Thursday to Friday night, so I was up when the steamer got into Albany, and could not have gone ashore even if Canterbury had have got leave.

Albany looked very nice from the steamer on Friday morning when the sun rose. It is something like Lyttleton to look at but the hills are nothing near as high and the place is not nearly so big, but as it is built on a slope it shows up very well from the harbour. The entrance is a good length, and as it bends about a good deal you can see no signs of the town until you get fairly into the port, when you see the town round a bend on your right.

Nothing of any importance happened on the Friday; those companies went away in the launch, and the others, excepting the ship's guard, which included me, had to scrub down decks and clean rifles, but we were eagerly looking forward to the morrow when our turn was to come to walk land once more.

Well, Saturday turned out a lovely day and at 5.30 No. 3 troop deck (ours) was the scene of some very quick movements in the way of getting down hammocks and rolling blankets. As everybody had to be cleaned up before breakfast and all the lower deck brushed and scrubbed, you can guess that we had to be pretty slippy.

I need not go into all the details of our morning's work; sufficient be it to say that half-past-eight found everything in first-class order and all of us in full rig with

Soldier Boy

polished boots, bright spurs and clean leggings to say nothing about smaller items, ready for the launch which drew alongside a few minutes later. It did not take us long to get aboard, I promise you, and then a five-minutes run brought us to the jetty. After being duly warned as to our conduct etc. we were dismissed and then the fun commenced.

About five more minutes brought us fairly into the town, and then commenced a well-organised rush on the post office. That over, the fruit shops and hotels began to feel the effects of khaki, but I must say that our squad behaved remarkably well in the latter respect.

It was very amusing to see the way the khaki lads scattered. They were all over the place in no time. The most notable thing was the number of them that took to riding bicycles. In less than half an hour there was not a machine to be had in town. All the shops were rushed as everybody wanted a spin once more after a fortnight on the ocean. As we were going to make the best of our time and lay in a store of odd things for the remainder of our voyage, each table had previously drawn up an order of such like things as jam, pickles, biscuits etc, so the head of each table could be seen strutting here and there into shops ordering in great style.

Our table put in three shillings per head, which meant a little over £2, so you will see that we were able to get a good few little necessaries. It was great fun to see the lads coming up the street in grand formation but rolling like tipplers and all complaining that the Australian soil was very unsteady.

I had a real good look around the place and I can truthfully say that for cleanliness it could not be beaten anywhere, and that is saying a good deal in the face of a place like Christchurch. The only thing the contingent boys have against it is the outrageous prices they charge for things. We all expected to see things very cheap there, but we were very much deceived as we had to pay 10d a pound for biscuits and the same for grapes, 1/3d for cake and 9d for apples, which seemed to us outrageous entirely. However, they paid us before we went ashore and so we did not mind so very much. We all looked on it as the last time we might be able to have a splash and so we splashed accordingly.

It did not take long for our four hours leave to go, and then started the business of getting once more over to the steamer. As I said before, it is a few minutes walk from the jetty to the town, and making for the launch could be seen squads of Tommies varying in size from three to a dozen, some carrying boxes and bags and such like. I got down to the boat before the most of them so had the pleasure (for a pleasure it was) of watching the human stream winding down and coming into the boat shed. It was quite a study, I assure, and needed no imaginative mind to give it all the charm of the wonderful.

First would come a couple of chaps carrying a large case with drops of sweat on their brow and a weary expression on their faces. Carefully they would deposit their burden, in fact, so carefully that the officers standing by would wink and give each other a knowing look which, as you may not see the meaning, was as good as saying that there was more than eatables inside, what more you may guess. Probably they were mistaken; let us hope that they were.

Next would come more chaps in a bunch, but a step above the last as they would have a porter to wheel their things for them. Then would come another fellow with something under his arm that did not look like a parcel and walking hastily, occasionally casting hurried glances over either shoulder. As he comes nearer we see that he has a cat under his arm which immediately explains the looking back and hurried step. He looks very pleased with himself and his capture when he gets safely into the shed. Then would come a bloke more fortunate than the majority who had a lady friend in the place and who now in her company was drawing near to the place of parting with that fixed expression of features and slow pace on his part and watery-eyed sorrowful look on hers which we learned to know so well in Wellington especially towards the end of our stay there.

I will not deal but turn my, and direct your, attention to the next single individual who also comes with a flutter, with a living 'something' under his arm, but at a run this time instead of a walk. As he draws nearer we see not a cat but a dog this time, and once more the carrier is perspiring. Holding his prize securely he glances round on his chums, and finally, having found his breath in a broken sort of way, he explains that "I prug this bloke up the street and a duce of a job I've had to get the fightin' little beggar here too," as he and the captured quadruped safely pass through the gate toward the sea.

So the stream continues until all are in and ready to embark. Others bring pets as well, and I may as well state here now that at present we have three dogs and seven cats aboard, besides several donkies (big 'uns).

It has just popped into my head that I omitted to tell you a thing or two about Albany niggers and a few of their doings, so before I pass on I will finish that little

Soldier Boy

item up. Well, we saw four in all and one wee spratt-nigger in arms. They were at street corners begging, two men and two women, if such a name can be applied to such objects. I have seen some specimens of Maories in the North Island but the worst I ever saw was a king to them. Both men and one of the women (a very old one) were dressed in kangaroo skins and you can guess their appearance when I tell you, and truthfully, that Old Hick would be fat compared to them, and both their person and their skin robes seem to call aloud for the intervention of a sanitary inspector. In fact, even yet you will hear chaps talking of them on board here and saying to each other "just weren't they specimens and gum, didn't they pong".

Well, one of the old men who introduced himself to us as King Billy made himself very much at home with us and in the course of his bungled conversation he let drop that he could throw the Boomerang and cunningly insinuated that a bit of coaxing and silver would soon bring him to do it for our edification. Nothing loth we subscribed and got the old chap a boomerang and gave him a few shillings to boot, and then the old bush fire came back to him or seemed to, for in a second he had thrown off his skins and was off down the slope with a step that greatly surprised us all for its spring, especially when we considered his hair and beard were white as could be.

The town where we were was something like what Ted Cooper's is, on top of a slope and flat at the bottom of a slope like Hassall's bank might, but with another road down where the line is. Supposing that there was a three-storied hotel in the place of Cooper's you about have the place exactly. We were on the top road, or street in this case, and he made off down the slope on to the bottom one. Seeing that he meant to throw the thing towards us and knowing the trick a boomerang is apt to play, we parted and tried to make room for it as we thought. We need not to have bothered, for catching it the way Will showed Louis he ran forward at an angle, a pace or two, and then let it go.

It may have been because it was coming up hill and towards us, but at first it did not seem to go so very quick, but gaining speed it shot over our heads and away it went in splendid style right over the hotel out of sight. We thought it was gone, but presently back it came like lightening over the road and down the slope, passing over Billy's head (mighty close it seemed but he stood perfectly still) and it landed six or seven yards behind him. I promise you we cheered the old fellow

The Gulf of Taranto, on which Harry sailed from Wellington to South Africa in late April, and at which time he wrote the first of his string of letters home. (GILBERT FAMILY COLLECTION)

as he came back up the hill. He came strutting back with the conscious air of superiority which at times niggers know so well how to assume. He would have liked to have thrown it again a time or two at the same rate of pay, but as a few more exhibitions would have been expensive and we had seen what he could do we were satisfied to thank the old chap and pass on, but it was easy to see that it was not the first time he had used the twisted stick.

Soldier Boy

Sunday 28th

Another week on the water and now I am going to put a bit more on to this. I may as well go back though and go on with my yarn where I left off, before I mentioned the darkies. Well, it didn't take us long to get ourselves on to the launch again but getting the boxes etc was a much longer business but amidst shouting and laughing and occasional forcible exclamations from those in charge it was at last safely accomplished, and with cheers ringing from the shore and the Warcry bellowing from the boat we start for our transport and bade goodbye to Australasia for the last time.

Nothing happened of interest. We were soon aboard and all goods and chattels with us and decks were cleared for the start for Durban. At half past three we weighed anchor and steamed slowly down the harbour towards the open sea once more. One of the local Artillery Corps was practising on the hills as we passed and their signalman up with his flag and waved "Good Luck" and "Godspeed" to us, to which our signallers on the bridge replied. So much for our stay in Albany.

When Sunday morning dawned we had left land far out of sight behind us and we won't see it again until we sight the African coast. I should have told you that just after dark on Saturday night we saw three steamers, one on our right and two on our left. Two were a good distance off, but one of those on our left was as close as they dared come at night time. I should think, and as the rumour got about among us that it was the returning Third and fourth. We cheered and shouted our "Warcry" we were hoarse. We were answered back from the stranger, but it did not strike us as coming from the throats of NZ lads and I guess we were mistaken about them, but we sent up rockets and coloured fires as we passed on and left them in the darkness astern.

About ten o'clock on Sunday morning we passed a school of whales. There must have been over a score of them sporting on the water away on our left, and "blowing" in all directions. They were too far away for us to examine them with our optics but they looked like big black logs on the surface of the water. We have seen no more sharks since we left Albany, but in spite of being a good deal south of the line we have seen flying fish wizzing round the boat sometimes. They are strange little beggars, not very big but they come out of the water with a splash and fly like the mischief for about a couple of chains, and just as you are about to lay heavy odds with your mates that they are birds, up comes their tails and closing their "wings" they disappear into a wave with another splash and are gone.

Having no horses on board we are having a very easy time of it; in fact too easy, for excepting a few sick ones we are all putting on weight and sometimes time hangs very heavy on our hands. However, we are not short of pastimes etc for we have draughts, deck quoits and other such amusements as Tug-of-war and cock-fighting. The way we go about it is this. First a big spar about seven inches in diameter is securely lashed across from the bulwarks to the main hatch about four feet above the floor, or deck I should say, then mattresses are spread underneath so that the fighters won't hurt themselves when they come off. Then two fellows, with a pillow in each hand climb up and with nothing to hold on to start and belt away at each other all they can draw. It is good fun I assure you, for what with a chap banging at your head and the rolling of the boat to contend with it is no easy matter to sit on a smooth round spar.

Our Captain (Coutes, who won the Queen's scarf for bravery in the Transvaal before) put us up to the game and he and our regimental Sergt Major started the exhibition with a go between each other. It was great sport but the Captain eventually vanquished his opponent, and since then the game has been very popular.

A very much needed thing was a bath, and that difficulty has been got over now by rigging up a sail in the form of a large tank and filling it with water. Now at reveille (6am) every man has to jump out of his bunk and scoot off up on deck for a dip and once the bath is full (ten get in at a time) the chaps belonging to the steamer turn the engine hose on the lot. The splashing and the yelling you can imagine better than I can describe.

We have a Church Parade forard every Sunday morning when it is calm enough. With what I have told you about our pranks, such as boxing and pillow-fighting you may think that we are a good-for-nothing lot but if you could have heard the hymns this morning and the response to such prayers as "We beseech Thee with Thine arm to strengthen us in the day of battle" you would not think so for long, I'm sure.

We have the Church of England service and Sankey's hymns as they are the best-known generally. The best known service is, or seems to be, the one we use.

The officers had a small paper printed at Albany, "The Budget" they called it. I am going to send you a copy from Durban if I can. It did not please us chaps, so we have started one on our own account called "The Despatch" and I have been put on the staff as one of the writers. We have no printer on board of course but we write a complete copy for each company and one for the officers and ship's Captain, so you will see that we have our hands full, while it lasts. We publish it every Saturday and we were going like mad to get yesterday's issue out, for when we were just fairly under way on Thursday night a big sea struck us fair broadside and in the roll that followed our pot of ink went flying sending the fluid over everything and among the rest, it spoilt 25 sheets of MS, much to our annoyance. We are going to have each issue printed when we get to Durban and I will send you some copies of it for comparison with "The Budget" and to send to the folks in England as a keepsake from me.

I think I have told you all the news up to date so I will stop and lay this aside for a day or two until something else happens. "Taihoa."

Friday May 3rd

I am going to try and add a bit more to this now so that I will have it about ready for the post by the time we reach Durban which won't be long now as we have reduced the distance to hundreds instead of thousands of miles. We reckon to reach there by Wednesday or Thursday if the weather holds good and just at present it is so splendid, in fact we have had no rough weather so to speak since we left Australia's coast. Just at present I suppose we are somewhere in the Indian Ocean, just where I don't know but we are on Line 80 South some place or other, with nothing but water everywhere, morning after morning just the same and it seems as though we have not moved in the night at all. It is easy to tell we are in a different climate now. The air seems different and the days are very hot considering the time of year. It is about 7 or half-past now and still all hands or nearly all are running about in their shirt sleeves, and although that way I am sweating down below here. Of course it is a bit cooler up on deck.

This is the greatest crew for petty larceny and practical jokes that ever I was amongst. Personally I have had my spurs, field service cap, one shirt and a towel lifted off me since I joined but I have recovered all but my spurs and cap which as yet, successfully elude my searches, but I'll get them (or someone else's) before I'm much older. In the line of practical jokes, letting down hammocks is very common and as a rule constitutes a huge surprise for the victim. Sometimes, in his sleep, a chap opens his mouth and begins to snore. That is a splendid chance for the worker of mischief. Swiftly he secures a pellet of soap and drops it into the offending sleeper's mouth and departs. What happens when the sleeper awakes (which is invariably mighty soon after the administration of the pill) in the way of rearing and spluttering I will leave untold.

Tickling sleepers' noses and feet with twigs are among the commonest of our capers, and going round with a bit of water in a mug and dashing it on such parts of slumberers as may be exposed is generally a very good way of raising a friendly skuffle (sic). I am not going to say that I don't take part in these things as I fear that I am oftener in than out of them. Everything is taken in good part though, as long as no one starts after lights out when we want to be asleep. If that is done, well things hum. Only last night after I was asleep a chap came and started on to me. First he tried to get into my bunk and hoist me out. That woke me up but did not work, then he started to worry my feet. A chap woke up out of a sleep is generally a rusty customer to fool with and I was no exception. I told him to stop and go back to bed before he got hurt, but he did not seem to see it and in reply gave me a wet rag in the face. I opened out as loudly as I dared then but a minute later he ran a cold empty bottle under the blankets and up my back. My Irish was up then, but I stopped still hoping that would be his last, but no, next thing whack came an empty bottle on to me. That was too much. In my rage I grabbed it round the neck, fairly heaved myself out of bed, and landed him over the head with it.

It was a dangerous thing to do and if I had thought a minute I would not have done it, but in moments like that a chap is not given to thinking. At any rate, it quietened him. I got to sleep and he got a big head and I anticipate a very good night tonight.

We saw a tremendous dose of flying fish today, the most we have seen together so far. They are strange little objects.

It is very comical to hear the different speeches that come from chaps who are going through their kits and discover some articles to be missing. The other day just after dinner things were fairly quiet for a wonder and suddenly out of the silence came a voice with "It's no bloomen' good the bloke who stole my towel must suffer, and the next clean one I see without a brand is mine." What connection there was between the two sentences and how he was going to make the man who stole his suffer, as he called it, by stealing somebody else's, he did not explain.

Soldier Boy

One witty chap commenting on this ever-going hoisting of things remarked that soon a chap will have the shirt stolen off his back and "when he lays himself down anywhere, when he comes back it will be ten chance to one if he doesn't find himself gone," so you see what a pitch things have reached.

Sunday May 5th 1901

I am going to put a bit more on to this now and that will be the last until I reach Durban which will be on Wednesday all being well. I have not got very much in the way of news to tell you as you have got just about all the ship's doing in the preceding pages, and at any rate after reading it this far, you may not feel inclined to decipher much more of my beetle-tracking. We are not so very far off the African coast now and all hands are getting their writing done up ready for landing as we will have very little time when we get ashore this time. It won't be a holiday trip like Albany was.

We have been ordered to have everything in our kits clean and packed by Tuesday night but I have all mine done except washing a pair of trousers and a shirt. When you write don't forget what I said in my last about long letters and don't be afraid to run into an extra stamp or two as I won't get many letters from NZ or any other place for that matter and the intervals between the arrivals of them won't be short. I did not get any letters in Albany and we won't get any in Durban as they won't be got there yet and when they do arrive we will be gone and they will have to follow us on to Pretoria.

It's five weeks now since I heard from Cust and a month since I had a letter from anyone else and I guess it will be as long again before I have another so you see I am not burdened with my letters at all. You must pass my letters round as I cannot write to all hands. I wrote to Joe from Newtown but although there was plenty of time for him to reply he never did it and so I suppose he and the rest of the NZ Gilberts have given me over to the bad. I never had so much as a note from any of them and they could easily have sent one by Whittas or Gillams who were both down to see us off, and they knew it, but no. It was not as if I had not written because I did, and Joe at least might have answered it.

I reckon it was decidedly unfair and I have not written since so they can't write now as they don't know where to send to, but it's all in a life time and with us now at any rate "Life's too short to quarrel". So they must gang their own with it. It was a dangerous thing to do & if I had thought a minute I would not have done it, but in moments like that a chap is not given to thinking. At anyrate it quietened him. I got to sleep & not a big head & I anticipate having a very good night tonight. We saw a tremendous dose of flying fish today the most we have seen together so far. They are strange little objects. It is very comical to hear the different speeches that come from chaps who are going through their kits & discover some articles to be missing. The other day just after dinner things were fairly quiet for a wonder & suddenly out of the silence came a voice with. "Its no bloomen good the bloke who stole my towel must suffer, & the next clean one I see without a brand is mine" what connection there was between the two sentences & how he was going to make the man who stole his, suffer, as he called it, by stealing somebody elses, he did not explain. One witty chap commenting on this ever-going hoisting of things remarked that soon a chap will have the shirt stolen off his back & "if he lays himself down anywhere when he comes back, it will be ten chances to one if he doesn't find himself gone," so you see what a pitch things have reached.

Sunday. May 5th 1901. I am going to put a bit more on to this now that will be the last until I reach **Durban** which will be on Wednesday all being well. I have not got very much in the way of news to tell you as you have got just about all the ships doings in the preceeding pages. & at anyrate after reading it thus far, you may not feel inclined to decipher much more of my beetle-tracking. We are not so very far off the African coast now & all hands are getting their writing done up ready for landing as we will have very little time when we get ashore this time it wont be a holiday trip like Albany was. We have been ordered to have everything in our kits clean & packed, so I must gait, but it's agranoyen. However, I hope 8000 miles of water won't keep some letters from reaching me.

May 9th

We arrived in Durban today but as yet we have not landed, only the Colonel and Captain going ashore. We saw a couple of whales the day before yesterday, sperm ones quite close and a tremendous size. As I said before our Colonel went ashore and he got us through the health officer I suppose for orders have come as follows: 7th will disembark at 9 tomorrow. At 12 they will entrain for Pietermaritzburg. There they will be fitted out with new uniforms and rifles etc and immediately proceed to the front. We don't know who the orders are from but they sound uncommonly like Kitchener we think. I have no time for more as we have to get everything ready by eight tomorrow and after five weeks on the water that means a lot.

There is a tremendous lot of shipping here. We are anchored outside and this is 15 steamers round us and in the harbour we can see quite a forest of masts but we will see it from close quarters tomorrow.

Remember me to all the people especially Mrs Cromie and Sarlies. I hope you are all well and not worrying too much about me. I have no time for more now, as I must write a few more lines to Jessica before I start to pack and as you can imagine things are in a large bustle, Transports, Store ships, Hospital ships, with their large red crosses showing mercifully clear and launches everywhere and a sullen man o war or two all around us. The CIV's [City Imperial Volunteers London] are anchored out here ready to start for home and the Warwick regiment is off them a little way. We asked by our signals our own, where they were going but all we could get out of them was that they had Boer prisoners aboard and were under sealed orders. They told us at the start of the war they came out of England 1100 strong and now they are going away with 250 men in the ranks. They are brave fellows.

Give my love to Annie and Perc and tell them that I haven't forgotten them nor the organ. I must stop now.

Best Love
Harry

It may well have been the sight of these Imperial troops seen here parading through the streets of Dunedin in early 1901 that inspired the young Harry Gilbert to join up soon after.
(COURTESY HOCKEN LIBRARY, DUNEDIN)

Transport Gulf of Taranto.
May 4th 1901

My Dear Father.

I am just going to write you a
few lines to go with Lotties. I have nothing
much to say as I have told pretty well all
in my family one which you must pass
round. I will keep it open & put in
the latest news before I post it in Dur
-ban. I told you before about leaving £1·1·0
behind me in the Ch. Ch. P.O. & I also told
you my Regimental number (4407.) We have
each sewn up small linen slips in our
war trousers. These contain our name & all
particulars & also the name & address of our
next of kin. Your name & address has been
filled in on mine. so in case of my being
picked off you will receive all my savings
& belongings such as I may have at the time
The reason these are worn will be perfectly
obvious to you without my tellin. I hope
you were well on your holiday round
Garfield etc & trust that you are still so.
Behind this I am putting a list of things
which we wear & carry on the march & in
closing must ask you to Write Soon to
            Your Aff Son
                H. G. Gilbert.

Our holdall is a sort of an with compartments for soap razors, tooth knife
fork spoon, tobacc pipe, & any more things which are wanted on the march
In fact we are to be like the cat who carry our all with us wherever we so
only we wont have tents like them very often mving mother earth & sky
for a bed & covering. Ill write when I can.

Transport Gulf of Taranto
May 7ᵗʰ 1901

My Dear Father

I am just going to write you a few lines to go with Lottie's. I have nothing much to say as I have told pretty well all in my family one which you must pass round. I will keep it open and put in the latest news before I post it in Durban.

I told you before about leaving £1.1.0 behind me in the ChCh PO and I also told you my Regimental number (4407). We have each sewn up small linen slips in our war trousers. These contain our name and all particulars and also the name and address of our next of kin. Your name and address has been filled in on mine so in case of my being picked off you will receive all my savings and belongings such as I may have at the time.

The reason these are worn will be perfectly obvious to you without my telling.

I hope you were well on your holiday round Darfield etc and trust that you are still so.

Behind this I am putting a list of things which we wear and carry on the march, and in closing must ask you to Write Soon to

Your Aff Son
HG Gilbert

Our holdall is a linen afair with compartments for soap, razor etc, comb, knife and fork, spoon, tobacco, pipe and any more things which are wanted on the march. In fact we are to be like the Arabs and carry our all with us wherever we go, only we won't have tents like them, very often using mother earth and sky for a bed and covering. I'll write when I can.

This last-minute addition appears in the left-hand margin of the letter.

Soldier Boy

On the flip-side of
Harry's single-page letter
to his father is this list
of equipment and other
detail:

Seventh Contingent New Zealand Mounted Rifles
Full Marching Order

Haversack   Worn over right shoulder

Water bottle   " " left "

Blanket   On rear of Saddle

Bandolier   Worn over left Shoulder

Overcoat   On front of Saddle

Canteen   " near side of overcoat

Nosebag   On near side D of saddle

In Near Wallet
Curry comb, Horse brush, sponge and soap, Horse rubber

In Off Wallet
Towel, pair of socks. Shirt or singlet. Hold all, Pair of drawers.
Built up ropes, Heel rope, picquet pegs strapped on great coat.
If rear pack is carried picquet pegs will be strapped thereon.

We carry 50 rounds of ammunition in our bandoliers and 100 in our
pouches on the march and 50 more when going into action, or near the
Boers. Our Canteens as I explained in Wellington, is a combination of a
frying pan, panikan and plate folding into each other. Built up ropes are
pieces of rope with a loop on one end and a short cross stick on the other,
so [illustrated]. Each a yard long and each trooper carries one so that at
night one long rope is formed in a minute. In addition to [the] above I have
a revolver so am well equipted for gear and have plenty to carry.

Twenth Contingent
New Zealand Mounted Rifles
Full Marching Order.

Haversack.   —   Worn over right shoulder.
Water bottle   "   " left.   "
Blanket
Bandolier   On rear of Saddle
Overcoat   Worn over left Shoulder.
Canteen   On front of Saddle.
Nosebag.   —   " near side of overcoat.
                On near side D of saddle.

In Near Wallet.
Curry comb. Horse brush, Sponge & soap. Horse rubber.
In Off Wallet.
Towel, pair socks, Shirt or singlet. Hold all
Pair of drawers,
Built up ropes. Heel rope, picquet pegs, strapped on
great coat. if rear pack is carried picquet pegs will
be strapped thereon.

We carry 50 rounds of amunition in our bandoliers &
100 in our pouches on the march & 50 more when going
into action, or near the Boers. Our Canteen as I explained
in Wellington is a combination of a frying pan, panikan
& plate folding into each other, Built up ropes are
pieces of rope with a loop on one end & a short cross
stick on the other so. o———◦ Sach a yard long &
each trooper carries one so that at night one long
rope is formed in a minute. In addition to above I
have a revolver so am well equipted for gear & have
                plenty to carry.

The Tommies are the best chaps in the world they would give away their shirts they help us in every possible way.

Dear Everybody

Just a few lines before we should shift up country a bit further. Excuse scribble as I [am] sitting on the ground in my great coat & writing these on a tin lid for a desk. We had a great time landing at Durban. I may have time to tell you later on some time but I have not now. We left there at half past five the same evening & travelled all night. We [left] only one company at Pietermaritzburg after all & the rest came on 50 miles further up to here. We had a scone & a mug of water each for dinner & left without a tea we were told that we would suffer up the line some where. As it turned out we did no[t] see a scrap until night then we stopped for a while at a station & were served out with a drink of tea & a hunk of dry bread [the] night was intensely cold & as you well know we were hungry so it vanished. Sleep was impossible so as [we] boomed along in the darkness we passed the night best we could by singing & making speeches. At last at six o'clock or a bit before just as day was beginning to break the train steamed into Mooi River. After unloading our baggage in the cold grey morning we marched out to the Cavalry camp here about a mile [from] the station. I have often wondered what a battle field was like & now here we are camped on one. Birth of

[Left margin, written vertically:]
...you may ask & don't worry. The days are very hot & the nights awful cold but we are on active service — we don't mind as ...then we can help it. We get hefty beef & biscuits when we can ...the biscuits. Goodbye. Larry

Mooi River Camp
May 14th 1901

Dear Everybody

Just a few lines before we should get a shift up country a bit further. Excuse scribble as I am sitting on the ground in my greatcoat and writing this on a tin lid for a desk.

We had a great time landing at Durban. I may have time to tell you later on some time but I have not now. We left there at half past five the same evening and travelled all night. We only left one company at Pietermaritzburg after all and the rest of us came on 50 miles further up to here. We had a sandwich and a mug of water each for dinner and left without a tea and we were told that we would supper up the line somewhere. As it turned out we didn't see a scrap until midnight and then we stopped for a while at a station and were served out with a drink of tea and a hunk of dry bread.

The night was intensely cold and as you well know we were hungry so it vanished. Sleep was impossible so as we loomed along in the darkness we passed the night as best we could by singing and making speeches.

At last at six o'clock or a bit before, just as day was beginning to break, the train steamed into Mooi River. After unloading our luggage in the cold grey morning we were marched out to the Cavalry camp here about a mile from the station.

I have often wondered what a battlefield was like and now here we are camped on one. North of us is the kopje where the Boers were stormed out by the Naval Brigade under Buller, and Northeast is the high hill where the Boers were driven out from their positions and big gun at the point of the steel. West of us lies an English General and on the ridge above the camp is the grave of a soldier and a Boer side by side. On the Englishman's mound is a rough cross with "Gone but not forgotten" on it. The Boer being wounded was left behind by his mates when they hurried off. The Englishman went up to help him and as he approached the other raised himself and shot him. As he fell he bayoneted the cowardly brute and there they lay side by side.

Clumps of ground and piles of fired off cartridges mark the spots where the fight was hottest, but enough of this.

Soldier Boy

In camp with us are the dragoons and the three or four lots of Hussars and one Reg of lancers. The day after we arrived we had a football match. The ground was marked out by flags on bayonets and the goal posts were lances 10ft long from the Tommies.

I can't give you the camp news, it would fill a book, but the Kaffirs are a never-failing source of amusement in thousands of ways. Everything here speaks of war. Trains by the score all day and night long. Ammunition and stores literally in mountains, soldiers everywhere. Just over from us is the remount depot. There they have 25,000 horses, 7000 in the one paddock. It is a big one being a few square miles of veldt. The Boers were hovering round this camp three weeks ago and we needless to say are keeping a strict watch night and day.

We have just got word that there is a commando a 1000 strong and we are to be in readiness to go at any minute so I must stop and join in the bustle. We will probably start North tomorrow morning. Remember me to all who may ask and don't worry.

The days are very hot and the nights are awful cold but we are on active service so we don't mind any more than we can help. We get bully beef and biscuits here. I am going to post you one of the biscuits when I can. Goodbye, Harry.

The "Tommies" are the best chaps in the world. They would give away their shirts and they help us in every way possible.

These last two sentences were added in a hasty three-line scrawl across the top of the page.

My Dear Mother

I'm just going to strip in a few lines along with Lottie's to let you know that you are not forgotten. As you will see by hers we have had another big shift again this time down South. If we keep on at the rate we are going we will know the Transvaal like a book.

We have been up Pretoria way round "Springs" close to Jahannasburg and down around the Free State in fact we have been travelling ever since we landed here and seeing strange country nearly all the time.

I hope you don't worry too much about our losses Mum. Someone must go you know and as for myself when my turn comes I will have to go too but I hope it won't be out here. If it is I trust you will be able to say of me that "He like a soldier fell" wherever it happens. I don't think the war can hang on much longer.

Excuse the style of this note. Same old tale no time to write well. If I don't write for some time now don't be alarmed as we are in a different part of the country and it may be a hard matter to get letters away.

Love to all from
Harry

Undated and written in pencil on both sides of a tiny sheet of paper measuring 9.5cm deep by 12cm wide, probably torn from a much larger sheet, this was obviously intended for inclusion with another letter. From the contents it seems likely it was written early in Harry's time in South Africa. On the back he wrote 12 lines across the width of the page, then turned it sideways and wrote another eight lines in a bigger hand over the top of the earlier lines.

Soldier Boy

The paper for this abridged letter appears to have been carefully sliced in half and then folded to form a small four-page sheet, each "page" measuring 13cm by 10cm.

Standaton May 19th 1901

I did not get the chance to post my first letter at Mooi River as we got another order countermanding the first and telling us to move off at once so I had to bring my letter on with me. We were supplied with horses at MR and we started north with everything that night at 8.30.

Before we moved off we all had to charge the magazines of our rifles in case of accidents and we had to sit with our arms between our knees all that night. It was very cold but we were in carriages so did not mind much.

I can't go into details of the journey. We reached Ladysmith next morning and had breakfast, the first food we had tasted since the morning before, and even then it only consisted of 3 biscuits and a small drink. I have not got time to describe Ladysmith or in fact any of the places we passed through. It shows plenty of signs of the terrible siege. Miles of brestwork and sand bags and scores of graves. In fact the whole of the North of Natal up to here is dotted with them.

We got away from there as soon as we could and again made up toward the front. We passed over several battlefields and at last in the afternoon sighted the far-famed Majuba Hill where the disaster was in 1881. It is a high place, very rough on the sides and flat on top like most hills here. It is not very far from the Ingogo Station.

I won't enter into its history but we get it in full out here. The Tommy who pointed it out to me said: "There it is. For G--- sake try and get in a stab for that place." That's how they feel about it out here.

A little further up we passed through the Laing's Nek tunnel. You know all about it. Only three weeks ago the Boers blew up a train there and the ends of the tunnel too. A little after that and just as night was coming on we passed out of Natal and over the Transvaal border. Then we stopped at a place called Charleston and had dinner at 6.30. We were hungry, and we got dry bread there and another bit of a drink of cocoa. Soon after dark we were put into trucks and started for here. Needless to say we were like sardines.

The last words our Captain said before the train moved off were: "Keep your rifles handy and your bandoliers full, lads. The sparrows may be flying tonight." That was enough to keep us awake again in spite of being that way all the night before. It's a strange feeling travelling on through the night at a snail's pace, for they dare not go fast, not knowing but for any minute the bullets may start to sing around one's ears.

With a few stoppages we kept on until about 2.30 in the morning and then we drew into a place I can't remember the name of. There we were told that in spite of all our precautions the Boer had got wind of our coming (we had not been allowed to speak to anyone except in uniform) and had fired on the last train which passed through. As trucks crammed full of men are a good target our Colonel thought best to wait until daylight, and told us we could have three hours sleep which we all needed so much. It was a clear frosty night, or rather morning, and bitterly cold but we spread our waterproof sheets on the frosty veldt and then our blankets and turned in. We slept, but what sort of sleep I won't say.

I have not had my clothes off for quite a while now. As the Boer are afraid of close quarters in daylight we reached here in safety and then started to get our horses out etc.

I had a rather lively time that night as I was put on to guard a wagon load of ammunition. There was 16 mules yoked in it and two kaffirs driving. We had not left the station long when in spite of what I could say the thick-headed darkies tried to take a short-cut and got stuck. At first they flogged the mules but it was no go and only after I threatened them somewhat forcibly with my bayonet and rifle could I persuade them to unload part of the cartridges.

When we had got out of that and had gone on for about half an hour I thought the camp must be a long distance away and as I was on my first trip I asked the niggers if they knew the way. It was a job to make them understand what I wanted to know, but after diverse shaking of my hands and head I got "Noea Thur" out of them. Here was a fix. This is not a nice place to be lost in at any time much less at night, with a precious load of ammunition and two kaffirs who you can't understand and who can't understand you. I had an attack of that feeling which makes chaps look to their cartridge belts and examine the locks on their shooting irons. I need not go into details for after cruising about for a while I reached here and was very pleased with myself when I gave over my charge to the quartermaster.

We have no tents with us and we have to sleep under the stars. I have some dandy mates in my section and we sleep two together and thus get the benefit of two pairs of blankets, waterproofs and overcoats and sleep as warm as toast. It's quite a nice sensation to lie on one's back with your head on your saddle and look at the stars when you wake up and be just gloriously warm while the frost freezes your breath.

where the disaster was in 81. It is a high place
very rough on the side & flat on top like most
hills here. It is not very far from the Ingogo
station I wont into into its history but we get
it in full out here. The Tommy who pointed
it out to me said "There it is for G— sake
try & get in a stab for that place." That's how
they feel about it out here. A little further on
we passed through the Laing's Nek tunnel
You know all about it. Only three weeks
ago the Boers blew up a train there at
the end of the tunnel too. A little after
that & just as night was coming on we
passed out of Natal & over the Transvaal
border. Then we stopped at a place called
Charlestown. & had dinner at 6:30. We were
hungry & we got dry bread there & another bit
of a drink of cocoa. Soon after dark we were put
into trucks & started for here. Needless to say we
were like Sardines. The last words our Captain said
before the train moved off were "Keep your rifles
handy & your bandoliers full lads the sparrows
may be flying tonight. That was enough to keep
us awake again in stead of being that way
all the night before. Its a strange feeling

I did not get the chance to post my last till
Mooi River as we got another order countermanding
the first & telling us to move off at once so I'm
bringing my letter on with me We were supplied
horses at M R we started North with ever-
that night at 8:30. Before we moved off we
had to charge the magazines of our rifles in
case of accidents & we had to sit with our rifles
between our knees all that night. It was very
but we were in carriages so did not mind.
I cant go into details of the journey. We reached
Ladysmith next morning & had breakfast the
first food we had tasted since the morning before & even then it only consisted of
biscuits & a small drink I have not got to
describe Ladysmith or in fact any of the places
we passed through. I saw plenty of signs of
the terrible siege. Miles of breastwork & sand
& scores of graves. In fact the whole of the line
of Natal up to here is dotted with them. We
away from there as soon as we could & again
made up towards the front. We passed on
several little fields & at last in the af—

British Camp, a few miles out of Ermelo

May 28ᵗʰ 1901

My Dear Father

As we have halted here for a day I am going to try and steal a few minutes and write you a few lines to let you know of experiences since we left Standaton. Well we left there on Monday 20ᵗʰ a week ago yesterday and since then have passed through a good bit one way and another.

Our column under Colonel Gray is something under 2000 strong. It is composed of the Queensland Imp Bushmen about 450. Ourselves 620 or thereabouts and part of a regiment of the Lancashire Infantry.

Then we have 4 heavy pieces of field artillery, 2 pom-poms and one light gun (Maxim) so you see there is a good deal of fighting gear with us. As we were intended for quick movements we have no tents with us and we sleep "out". I have not had my clothes off or slept under canvas since I left Mooi River.

We did not advance very far on the first day and that night we camped at a place called Cralspruit. On Tuesday our scouts and some of the JTBs were fired on by the Boers for the first time but no damage was done except a bit of a scare for the ones who for the first time heard the bullets whistling. I was up all that night on Cossack post, as outlying sentry is called, but I was not fired on.

Wednesday morning we moved off pretty early but met nothing until late in the afternoon when we were fired on by the Boers from a kopje about a mile away as we were going into camp.

On Thursday No. 1 and 2 troop of Canterbury Coy (I am in No. 2) were advance guard and we were scarcely a mile and a half out of camp when heavy firing started on our left rear. A few minutes later it broke out on our right front so things were pretty lively for a time. However we did not slacken our pace but advanced steadily and soon the Boers were driven back in both places and we heard no more of them except a few sniping shots occasionally. No one was hurt in either place.

Nothing of any importance happened on Friday, we continued the march and on Saturday a little bit after dinner we drew up a mile outside of Ermelo.

That is a pretty looking little place not big enough to call a town and entirely deserted. It is strange to walk about a place where there is not a soul except the

This letter was written on small folded sheets similar to those used in the previous letter, with the pages irregularly numbered and the writing, in pencil, small and tight.

Soldier Boy

Tommies who are on guard. We secured a few things there. I got some Boer letters, cheques etc which I am going to send you with this if I can. (A third troop of Canterbury Rifles has just been ordered out and are off now for something). On Saturday evening we got orders that we were to make a night march at half past eight. That meant a good deal of bustle and to make things worse in the midst of it all up came a thunder storm. I have seen some lightning in NZ but not a patch on this. It rained very heavily for a while and then passed over.

When we were just about ready the order was altered from half past eight to half past twelve. As we all had to wait in full dress sleep was impossible and at last when the time came we were marched out of camp in the darkness. That was half after twelve.

No one was allowed to smoke or speak above a whisper. Only the mounted troops and two or three pieces of artillery were taken. Baggage was left behind as we wanted to travel fast.

It was very strange to see a thousand mounted troops going over the veldt in absolute silence except for the rattling of the bits. We had to pass over a range of hills on the very rough track and as a good many, myself included, went to sleep in the saddle some very pretty spills were the result.

All went well for a few hours until just as Sunday morning was dawning the first shot was fired from a farmhouse in front of us. A few minutes later our scouts opened fire and soon shots were going merrily all along the ridge. We retired into shelter for a time to let the guns, which were in the rear, come up, then we climbed nearly to the top of the hills and waited.

In the meantime one of our officers rode out to have a look at things. In a few minutes he came back and shouted to our Colonel for two troops of mounted men. Then came the order "Canterbury No 1 and 2, stand to your horses. Mount. Forward. Extend from the centre to 10 yards between files. Gallop." and we were off.

We charged round the nose of the kopje, over the side and made straight for where we thoughts the Boers were. We saw some away in front of us and came up to them at top speed. There was about twenty in all but some were mounted and got away but three of them down with their rifles and up with their hands as soon as we came up to them. They are great cowards.

We secured the three and for fear that the others were trying to lead us into a trap we were ordered to retire. Back we went and joined the main column and then we all advanced together.

A little later we saw the Boers who escaped the first time trying to get away up a sort of gully and my troop was ordered out again. We were soon hot after them again and as we went down a slope the pom-pom came into action and sent some shells whistling over our heads at the Boers beyond. As we were crossing a very bad spruit Billy Smith got a fall and I came nearly the same thing. The bank was so steep that his horse turned a summer salt backwards with him and I only saved myself from a similar spin by pulling my horse over sideways.

Neither of us were hurt but my horse was already lame as he came down into a springbok hole with me in the first charge and strained his leg. Smith's horse was done and the struggle finished mine so there was nothing for it but to return to the column. As we could hear them fighting in front of us we did not like to do this but we had to, however I need not go into the details of the rest of the fighting. Shots were exchanged all day.

We captured 12 Boers but did not kill any as the cowardly brutes would fire at us like mad while they were in a safe position but as soon as we dismounted to get a crack at them up would go their hands and they would give up the sponge.

One of our chaps was shot. Poor chap he only joined us at Standaton from the fourth. He could have gone home with them if he had liked but he chose to stay and join us. Maybe he is better off. We hope so anyway. We buried him soon after he was killed and so fell the first of the NZ Seventh.

I had to walk all the rest of the day so what with that and the night march I was tired enough, but my luck was out for that night I had to be up again on horse guard.

Yesterday there was no fighting only a bit of sniping round about but already we have got so used to the crack of the rifles that we take little or no notice of stray shots. Last night I looked forward to having a real good sleep but once again I was deceived for I had to go on outpost. The Boers are very fond of shooting the outpost sentries but last night not a shot was fired at me although the other side of the camp was fired on.

Already we have been away from Standaton longer than we expected to be and as we have prisoners to feed we are on three-quarter rations, that is three biscuits a day and get the rest where you can. Very often we don't get it, but when we can we

Soldier Boy

commandeer the Boers' sheep and cattle and thus get a bit of meat. When we can't get any we get meele and pumpkin and thus satisfy our inner man though raw pumpkin takes a bit of getting used to, but I can eat it now flying. If ever I get back to NZ I'll have some square feeds to make up for all this fasting I'll bet. This day's spell is very acceptable to most of us as we are dead tired. I'd sooner be sleeping now than writing but you will be wanting letters I know. You must excuse pencil and small writing for reasons that must be obvious to you – I cut the paper small so that I can put it in my diary and write a bit when I can. It is much handier than big sheets. In fact what with the wind and fellows tumbling about to write big sheets is impossible.

It was not uncommon for Harry to illustrate the envelopes of the letters he wrote home. The illustration in the bottom left-hand corner of this particular envelope incorporates his regimental number, "4407".

Monday June 3rd

Here we are again in Standaton or near enough to it as we are camped a mile or so outside of the town. We arrived here yesterday at 2 o'clock and mighty glad we were to get here too as we were just about on starvation rations. Two biscuits a day and half a pint of coffee.

I need not tell you how pleased we were to get six biscuits handed round and half a tin of bully beef with a tin of jam for four. It was quite a feast time last night I assure you. Long before this you will have seen by the papers what we have been up to. We have had a tough time of it. Fighting nearly every day. I can't go into it in detail. Last Friday and Sat was the worst. We had three killed and two wounded, one seriously and he is not expected to recover. He was shot in the stomach. The other had a thumb shot off.

It's a hard life sleeping out all nights and turning out at 4 in the morning and tending to your horses and saddling up in the stinging frost with the stars shining and then times and again moving out without any breakfast. Yesterday was a bitter day. I never in all my life felt cold so much.

We expected a spell here but hear that we are to start again on Wednesday. A lot of our fellows have gone into the hospital and one Queenslander died of enteric the day before yesterday. Anyone could combat disease if they could keep their insides full but as it was well you couldn't as we had to make 8 days rations last a fortnight.

For my own part I am keeping alright. I have not got a scratch in spite of the wizz ping of the bullets and am in good health but it is sad to see big men torn to pieces with dysentry. One fellow here now is walking about on sentry with his trousers all slack waiting for the next attack. I will stop now and write a bit to Mother.

Appallingly tough and tasteless into the bargain, the army biscuits Harry and his soldier mates had to gnaw on were often all that was available during their days out on the veld.

Your Aff Son
HG Gilbert

Soldier Boy

Note at the top of this letter: had 3 killed on Saturday and two wounded, 10 captured but released.

My Dear Mother

I have not got time or paper to write you much but I thought that I would just send you a few lines to let you see that I have not forgotten you. As I told Dad we arrived here safely yesterday after a fortnight of hard going. We were very glad to get back on to full rations again if nothing else. It's a hard thing to be hungry in the bush.

I used to think fried bread mighty short commons but we always had as much of it as we wanted and here we can't even get fried bread let alone half as much as we want. It's all for King and Country though.

Of course you will say all this serves me right and so it does I know, but that don't make it any nicer, as the Tommies say.

Out here we see the real Tommy, not the Dandy Dick type like we saw in town. They are splendid fellows in a good many ways, always ready to lend a hand and as brave as lions.

Have no time for more now, will send more when I can. In the meantime don't think too hardly of

Your Soldier Boy
Harry

Vereeniging SA
July 26ᵗʰ 1901

My Dear Mother

I am going to try and write you a few lines from this place in case you should not get the note I sent from Wolvehoek last week. I hope it will reach you before this one all the same but we never know where things go to in this country so it may never see NZ but even if it does I suppose it will make this none the less welcome.

We left Wolvehoek yesterday week and after trekking about a bit in the Free State, or Orange River Colony as it is called now, we crossed once more over the Vaal River and into the Transvaal. Apart from the fighting part of the business we have been having roaring times since then in the way of luxuries.

My Dear Mother

You may wonder at this but the part of the country we were in had not been visited by a British Column for seven months so besides Boers or "Jackies" there was plenty of fowls and pigs running about. These of course were our victims and added to this we had to clear a range of hills (the Losbergs) in which there was plenty of orange and lemon groves just loaded with splendid big ripe fruit. How we shone here I need not mention but the way we swarmed up the trees and the yellow cricket balls came down would make the onlooker think that we had been used to picking oranges all our lives. We have been living high and no mistake, four of us had 16 fowls between us one night and as many oranges as our skins and nose bags would hold.

We awfully annoyed our poor old Colonel one day (the Imperial one I mean, not Porter, he wouldn't have cared). Two hundred of us New Zealanders had been sent out with two big guns to do a bit of hunting when we came across a splendid patch of orange trees just loaded with fruit. After being on the baking veldt, where there is not a tree to be seen, a chance like this was not to be missed, especially with such a lack discipline lot as we are so off we made for a feed. Very nearly half the squadron were lost in the trees in a few minutes, many (a good many) without permission, and when the Colonel ordered an advance to be made my brave comrades were making a spirited attack on the standing fruit shop and Boers for the time being were forgotten and clean out of the list.

How he did perform. It was a treat to see him and his eyes as we came back with stomachs, pockets, hats, jerseys, nosebags and rifle buckets crammed full of yellow oranges. I personally was back in time to hear him say: "That's the way with these Colonials. Why don't you officers look after your men? Here we go out to do a certain thing, and all goes well until we reach a farmhouse where there is fowls or oranges or some other (adjective) thing of the like and then by Jerusalem, without a word the whole (another adjective) squadron falls out. Fall in you men who are back and let's get out of this." Such is the life we have been having this past week.

The Colonials are looked upon by all as "Tough members" and one English officer who it seems would know says that the New Zealanders are the "Worst disciplined, the best fighters, and (mark this but don't believe it) the biggest thieves" while our commander says the we ride and fight like the D---- in the day time and then sit up all night to cook and eat fowls or pigs as the case might be.

I must write a bit to Dad now so with the best love to all and wishing to be remembered to Mrs Cromie, Alice and the Earlys I Remain Your Aff Son
HGG

Vereeniging
July 26th 1901

Dear Father

I am going to put in a little bit for you along with Mother's just to give you a small idea of what we have been up to this last week since we left Wolvehoek. I have told her a bit about the best side of how we have been living and now I am going to tell you a little of the other side of the question and let you see that the Seventh has been taking its share of the hardships and fighting since we landed.

Well, when we left Wolvehoek we were told that there was a tough time before us as the hills we had to clear had not been visited by a column for seven months. We left on Wednesday and on Thursday we got another taste of fighting but nothing serious. On Friday we got in touch with a good number and our scouts in particular had a tough fight in front while our (Canterbury squadron) did a good job in the left flank. Canterbury had none hit but the scouts were not so fortunate. The Boers had them at a big disadvantage being hidden among the scrub on the banks of the Vaal and our men were in the open. However as soon as the Boers opened the duel our fellows nothing loathe dismounted and got at them. They had a tough go for a time but in spite of everything I am glad to say at last they drove the Jonnies out of their positions and over the river. How many Boers were hit is not known but the Scouts had three horses shot dead, three hit in various places, and three men hit. One, who was my bed mate before he joined the Scouts was shot in the arm, another through the calf of the leg, while a third was struck but not hurt much. As you will hear more about him in a minute I will tell you his name. It is George Darling. He is a very daring chap but for luck he beats all. We all wear two bandoliers now, one over the left shoulder and one for a belt round the waist and each holds fifty rounds. Well, he was laying down pelting away when whizz came a bullet and struck his full bandolier. It passed through that and his clothes exploding seven bullets in its course and continued its journey on and came out through the backside of his pants at last. How it did it without killing him is another of this country's marvels. His clothes were a good bit burned but next day he was fixed up and at it again as merry as a cricket. So much for Friday's work.

Saturday we moved off without much bother and went into camp after doing about 10 miles. Sunday morning we were roused out at 2 in the morning and 80 of us mounted and two guns moved out at something to four to surprise a party of Boers who were supposed to be sleeping in a farmhouse. They were too wide awake for us early as it was for they managed to get away. The way we went to get them was back on our old track and while we were searching about among the hills lo and behold we spotted a Boer convoy which was coming along the way we had come a day or two before. Our big guns came into action mighty quick and after a sharp tussle we got all the lot of the wagons and a lot of the women and kids. Most of the men galloped away and escaped but they left ten killed behind and we took 28 prisoners. The scouts who came on to some more of the wagons about three miles further down the stream scared the Boers away and when they were fairly going among their capture the Boers returned with reinforcements and our chaps had to go for their lives. Strange to say we did not have one man hurt that day.

The scouts told us that the wagons they saw could not possibly get away as they were blocked in a bad drift so the next morning we were out at half past three with two guns and a pom pom to catch the rest as we thought but we were greatly deceived. When we got to the drift in question the wagons were gone and the Boers had taken up a strong position in the hills.

We got to work on them and bombarded them for 2 hours with two fifteen pounders and a pom pom but failed to shift them. We had 10 wounded and one has since died. Our plucky Sergt Major was shot through the inside and is in a serious condition. You will know how he is long before you get this, his name is Callaway and he is from Auckland.

I must hurry up as orders have come out that we move in an hour to try and oust them from the position they have taken up. I believe that we are to take a 5 inch Howitzer to fire by so we will have a go before you get this. I must stop now.

Your Aff Son
Harry

Our capture on Sunday was 1045 bullocks, 800 treck oxen, 38 wagons, 15 cape carts, 800 sheep, 25 rifles, 2000 rounds ammunition and 200 horses.
Adieu

Vet Kop Lyndeque Drift July 22nd 01

The two stars are the passes we had to go through
No. (1) is where we were fired on first & where
our guns came into action
No (2) is where our guns opened fire from after we
had moved up, No (3) where the pom pom was in
action all the time. No (4) a low lying stretch
of bushes where Canterbury Co. doubled to No (5)
is the ridge where our horses took cover & where we
doubled out from. No 6) is an open flat where
Peterson & Trotter were shot. Callaway was shot
down by the bushes No (4). No 7 is a track
leading back from the Boer ridge & by
which they probably went away. No (8) the road
we came by No (9) a high Koppi where the Boers
tried to take position but were shelled off.

Harry wrote to his father in some detail about the battle above the Vaa River, in which his
regiment was involved in a tough and dangerous skirmish with Boer forces.

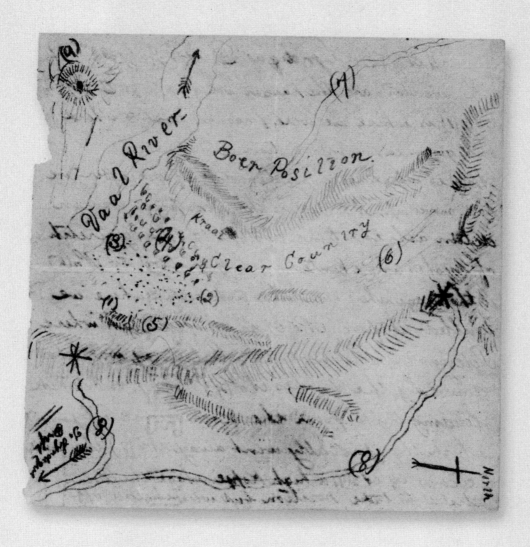

On the reverse of the scrap of paper on which he recounted the details of the battle, he drew this map of the scene along with their fighting positions, all numbered.

Outside of Kroonstadt, Orange Free State
August 2nd Friday

Written in pencil, this letter is on a scrap of paper 10cm wide by 14cm deep, seemingly torn from a larger sheet, perhaps the bottom right-hand corner from a notebook.

Dear Mother

Just a bit to go in with Louis'. I could not post his at the last place we passed (Potchfstrom) as we did not send a mail in but as we are going into Kroonstadt tomorrow morning I will get it away then if I can. I am expecting a dose of letters from NZ there as I have not heard from any of you for nearly two months. The last three mails has brought nothing for me although there was plenty for most of the others. I hope I'm not forgotten.

200 of us mounted men and 2 guns were routed out at 3.30 this morning to surprise some Jackies and now we are giving our horses a spell so I am sitting on my saddle in the veldt with the sun shining down on me mighty warm trying to scribble a bit to go "over the sea". You must excuse dirt I can't help it. Have slept on the ground every night for the last three months nearly and have not had my clothes off once in all the time except to change which I have done twice in that time. At present I am dirty as a sweep and ragged as a waif but in "Good foighten spirut" as paddy says and I would need.

We are in the Free State again now. I don't know what for. All of us who did the fighting in here last trick have had our names sent in for an extra bar on our medals so that's something. If I don't come back see that you get it won't you as we have earned it. I must stop now. If you have not answered any of my letters by the time you get this I hope you will send something if it's even a line as it's mighty stale out here week after week with no news at all.

Goodbye till next time.

Your Aff son
Harry

In Kroonstadt, August 3rd

Dear Mother

The mail did not leave camp last night as was stated in orders and as we came on today and got in here two hours ago I am just dropping you a line or two extra so that as far as I am concerned you will have the latest.

Us New Zealanders have got permission to cart a piano with us so every night now at the end of the horse lines comes sweet music. Our captures for July were 51 men, 50 Rifles, 84 wagons, 9,160 sheep, 3,082 cattle, 392 horses, 13,000 rounds of ammunition, 32 cape carts, 20 tons forage, 50 tons of mealies, 610 women and children, 460 Kaffirs. Not so bad for our column, was it, and not 2000 men all told.

Goodbye now, I must to work.

Yours As Ever
HGG (I wrote to Beckey)

Transvaal
Vereeniging
21st Aug 01

Dear Father

    I am going to try & write you a
few lines from here as I have not written you
a letter for a good while now. Since my
last was written at Kroonstad in the
Orange River Colony, late Orange Free
State we have travelled a good distance &
done a little more work in which I have
knocked my horse up completely so I am
here with some others who like myself have
been sent away from the Column to get
remounts. I did not half like leaving the
rest of the "Boys" as it is the first time
I have been off the veldt since we have
been on the trek In that respect I have
beaten all the lads who came from Cust
or thereabouts. Billy Smith went into

keeping up the line we went into camp
at a place called Honningspruit. You
can imagine how we felt at 4 on Sat
afternoon when orders came out that
250 of us et &c who had the best horses
were to move out at a quarter to seven
along with some Queensland Imp. Bushmen
for a night march. We got our horses fed,
saddled up, snatched a bit of tea (with
apologies) & prepared for 'bother'. Rifles
were cleaned, & our rations got together.
For the sake of our horses we were only
allowed to carry one blanket so we knew
what to expect. At a quarter to seven this
flying squadron moved out accompanied
with one pom pom. I need not go into a
detailed account of the march. You can
imagine a little bit what its like. Horses
falling into holes & chaps who think to
better themselves by walking falling into
holes themselves. In this way we kept

Imagine a
picture of
all the early
history of the
Transvaal.
It will make
some work for
four glass

Transvaal, Vereeniging

21ˢᵗ August 1901

Dear Father

I am going to try and write you a few lines from here as I have not written you a letter for a good while now. Since my last was written at Kroonstadt in the Orange River Colony, late Orange Free State we have travelled a good distance and done a little more work in which I have knocked my horse up completely so I am here with some others who like myself have been sent away from the Column to get remounts.

I did not half like leaving the rest of the "Boys" as it is the first time I have been off the veldt since we have been on the treck. In that respect I have beaten all the lads who came from Cust or thereabouts. Billy Smith went into hospital after our first trip to Ormelo and Pat Condon went in just after we got out here and before we had been on the veldt. After our second trip out that way Andie Russell knocked up and had to go into depot leaving Spencer and myself to fight it out about who should be last. However, when we got to Ventersburg Road his horse was done so he had to leave us, thus I was left, out of all the Cust boys on my own among about 500 other New Zealanders if such a term can be used.

It was not for long though, for that's not much over a week ago and here I am too, among the "Depot Scouts" or "Vereeniging Guards" as we are called, though that may not be for long either, we never know. It won't do any of us any harm for compared with the rations we get with the column we are living like "sons of kings" here and we have absolutely nothing to do until our horses arrive. It's fine to be able to lay in every morning just as long as you like after being rooted out at anything from 2 to four in the mornings for the last three months.

We were supposed to go to Bloemfontein when we left Kroonstadt the first time but after we had been out a few days we struck so many Boers and so much stock that after we had commandeered it all we were forced to put into the railway to get rid of it so we trecked back to Ventersburg Rd. and from there came on to Kroostadt again. We got in there on Thursday and of course we reckoned on a bit of a spell, but no next morning at 4 we were bundled out again and at daylight moved through the town up the line to a place called Jordan.

On the front page of this letter, Harry added a quick note, written at right-angles to the rest of the writing: "Am sending a picture of all the early men of the Transvaal. It will make some work for your glass" [see page 50].

47

Soldier Boy

On Sat. morning it was at 4 again and still keeping up the line we went into camp at a place called Honningspruit. You can imagine how we felt at 4 on Saturday afternoon when orders came out that 250 of us NZ'rs who had the best horses were to move out at a quarter to seven along with some Queensland Imp Bushmen for a night march. We got our horses fed, saddled up, snatched a bit of tea (with apologies) and prepared for "bother". Rifles were cleaned, and our rations got together. For the sake of our horses we were only allowed to carry one blanket so we knew what to expect.

At a quarter to seven this flying squadron moved out accompanied with one pom pom.

I need not go into a detailed account of the march. You can imagine a little bit what it is like. Horses falling into holes and chaps who think to better themselves by walking falling into holes themselves. In this way we kept on through the night. Several chaps went to sleep on their horses and fell off heels over head. I went to sleep myself more than once but I managed to keep my seat, though on one occasion I woke up and found myself and my horse wandering on our own.

It was a clear cold night and towards morning was simply freezing. At a quarter past four, as we were near the Jackies we halted and the scene then would take a better pen than mine to describe. Personally I was no sooner on the ground than I went to sleep where I stood and fell like a post into some other chap who was as bad as myself. Blankets were hastily unrolled and all hands laid down on the hard road to get a few minutes rest.

You know how horses are after a journey, but we could not help that; there we lay with the bridle in one hand and our rifle in the other, men and horses, which were as tired as we were, all huddled up together, amid the water and the dung, and the air, well, chilly.

Soon as the first streak of dawn put in an appearance, and just when we had laid long enough to get frozen and stiff, bang goes a rifle and then we know that our Sunday's business was started. When I got up, my horse, which had been lame all night, could not move so I had to hand her over and get another which was being led behind in case of emergencies. Rifles were now going lively all along our front and on the left front in particular.

I know that particulars of fighting do not interest any of you so I will pass that over and only say that we took 75 ponies, 5 wagons, 8 Cape Carts, 6000 rounds of ammunition, 41 rifles, with 25 prisoners and 2 Boers killed.

The fighting no one thinks so bad while they are in it but after it is over is the worst time. Most of the Boers seemed only too pleased to surrender but one would not give in though he was told to put up his hands about six times so they had to shoot him. Poor chap his bravery was worthy of a nobler cause. When he fell the chap who shot him went over, and he (the Boer) asked for a drink of water. No water could be got, but our chap handed his water bottle which was full of coffee and the Boer drank that. He only lived about 20 minutes for he was dead when the ambulance wagon reached him.

Soon as he was brought in our hardened old Colonel strides up and asks the doctor, "Where's that fellow who was hit this morning?" "He's here sir," says the doctor "He's dead now." "Hump," says the Colonel. "Dead is he? Got a pick or a spade about?" A statement which had only one meaning at a time like that.

A couple of niggers were sent to dig a grave, if such a hole could be called by that name. Looking down on his corpse one could not help but realise the possibilities of the life we are living. He did not seem to have suffered much for he lay with his right hand lightly clasping his clothes over his chest while his left was under his head which was turned slightly to the right. He was wrapped up in an old blanket which was pinned together with horseshoe nails, and with the warm blood still flowing slowly from the bullet hole he was placed in his grave. It was exactly the same as burying a dog. Not a word of service. Simply put him in a hole about eighteen inches deep and shovel the dirt on top of him, and even then his toes were left sticking out but that does not count out here.

I'll never forget the scene for along with many another it has made a lasting impression on my mind. I suppose it was about eight o'clock or half-past and the morning sun was just pleasant and warm. He was carried from the ambulance wagon to his grave on a stretcher with not a friend to follow or mourn him. Round the grave were a good many of us chaps with dirty faces, feathers flying in our hats and in a good many cases with our coats off and sleeves up, with our bandoliers next our shirts and leaning on our rifles without a word, our eyes alternately wandering from the still face and blood stained clothes of the Boer to the Kaffirs who were putting the finishing touches on the grave so hastily prepared.

It was a strange scene and seemed out of place on a morning so peaceful. However it was soon over and without even an "Ashes to ashes, dust to dust" or a

D SQUADRON 7ᵗᴰ N.Z.M.R. №1.

Members of D Squadron from the Seventh New Zealand Mounted Rifles, referred to by Harry as "all the early men of the Transvaal". Harry himself is the one in the broad-brimmed hat, second left in the second-to-front row. (Gilbert Family Collection) friendly tear to fall for him, he was left to rot under his native veldt.

The other Boer was shot at long range and as time was precious he had to lay where he fell. Such is the fate these Boers are daily earning by their wilful ignorance and stupidity, blinded as they are by such rascals as Steys, De Wit, and Botha, but it can't be for many months longer at the rate we are going.

Kitchener has issued a Proclamation which you no doubt have seen, and this is already making a difference though there are some who nothing will make surrender except a Lee Enfield bullet.

Of course the next thing to do was to get back as quickly as possible to the railway with our prisoners. As we were leaving about a dozen Jackies were seen sneaking round on our flank but a string of shells from the pom pom made them alter their minds and get. We travelled on in the heat and dust until half past seven that night, when we struck a station and our column's camp (which had in the meantime moved up the line) at a place called Rhenoster River. (Just ask Tom Dorn if he knows where that and Rhenoster Kop is, and see what he says.) We were glad to get between the blankets that night but next morning it was four o'clock again so you won't wonder when I tell you that we are always tired.

We dismounted fellows were sent on to here this morning. We came on to Vredefort Road, through Viljoens drift and at last arrived at Vereeniging. Here we get plenty to eat and can lay in as long as we like and here I have had the privilege of taking off my leggings, boots and clothes for the first time since I have been in the Transvaal. It is a treat though the ground hurts your bones a lot more when you're undressed, but that passes away with the arrival of sleep.
I must stop now.

Love to all from Your Aff Son
Harry

Sofsburg Hills
August 26th 1901

This abridged letter, written in ink, covers a total of 16 pages – four sheets of lined paper folded in half and written on all sides. On the last page Harry filled the page with writing from top to bottom, then turned the page sideways to conclude the letter.

My Dear Old Sis

As I have a bit of a chance I am going to try and answer your long and welcome letter which I received some time back at Ventersburg Road. You must excuse all the mistakes and scribble as writing has to be dashed off in a great hurry out here. As you will see by Dad, I was sent into depot at Vereeniging but I did not get the chance to stay long, as we were supplied with remounts and ordered to join our column at once on the same day as I finished his letter so I was only off the veldt one whole day.

Our detachment moved out of the town, if it could be called such, at dinnertime and we got into our column's camp, which was at a place called Reitspruit, about dark that night. Even though we knew that there was no more square feeds or rest for us for a while, we were not sorry to be once more with the "boys" after the Jackies.

We made a good start for next morning as per usual we were ordered out at 2 in the morning to get after a Boer convoy which was making for the hills. There was a good bit of fighting that day. There was two New Zealanders killed, Lieut Reece, and Sergt Major Love, both shot dead and one Queenslander, and Sergt Major Locket, of our Wellington Coy wounded. The Sergt. Major was shot through the right arm near the shoulder and he has since had to have it off. It's tough luck for him. We are getting up a subscription to send to Mrs Love who is in Wellington. It will be a hard blow for her.

Last night another of our officers died of some disease or another and he is to be buried today and another chap named Geo Clea, who was on duty last night at ten o'clock was carted over to the hospital at two this morning with a dose of Malaria fever, but he may get better. Altogether we are leaving a good number of graves scattered over the veldt. One out near Ormelo, three at Kaffirspruit, near Klipfontein, one at Standerton, one at Watervaalhoek one out Bethel way and now two at Reitspruit – besides leaving another man's arm there.

On the last day's fighting we got 8 prisoners, 8 wagons, 8 capecarts, 63 treck oxen, 162 cattle 16 horses, 3000 sheep, 8 rifles 500 rounds ammunition. How

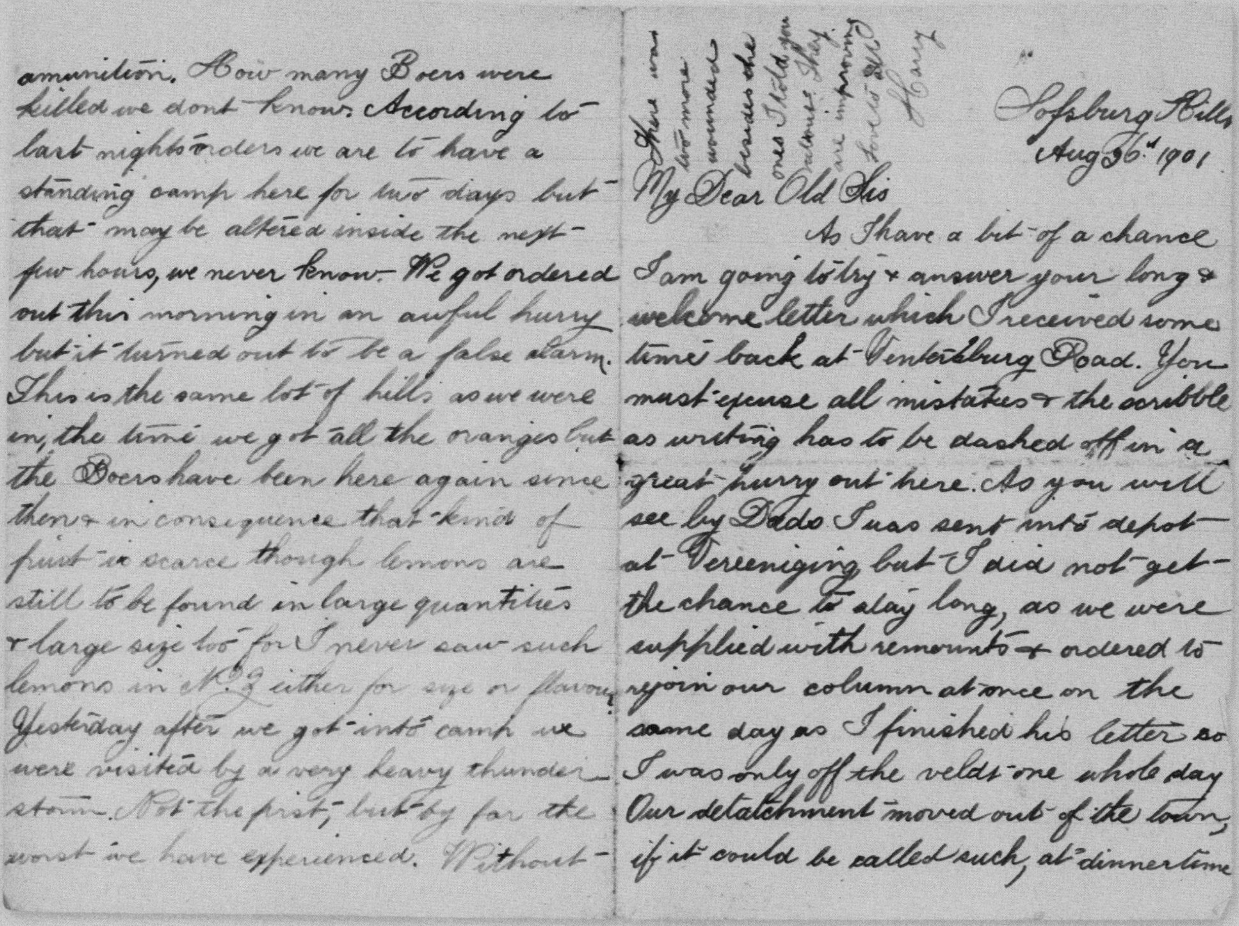

amunition. How many Boers were killed we dont know. According to last nights orders we are to have a standing camp here for two days but that may be altered inside the next few hours, we never know. We got ordered out this morning in an awful hurry but it turned out to be a false alarm. This is the same lot of hills as we were in, the time we got all the oranges but the Boers have been here again since then & in consequence that kind of fruit is scarce though lemons are still to be found in large quantities & large size too for I never saw such lemons in N.Z. either for size or flavour. Yesterday after we got into camp we were visited by a very heavy thunder-storm. Not the first, but by far the worst we have experienced. Without-

Lofsburg Hills
Aug 26th 1901

My Dear Old Sis

As I have a bit of a chance I am going to try & answer your long & welcome letter which I received some time back at Ventersburg Road. You must excuse all mistakes & the scribble as writing has to be dashed off in a great hurry out here. As you will see by Dads I was sent into depot at Vereeniging but I did not get the chance to stay long, as we were supplied with remounts & ordered to rejoin our column at once on the same day as I finished his letter so I was only off the veldt one whole day. Our detatchment moved out of the town, if it could be called such, at dinnertime

There was two more wounded besides the ones I told you about. They are improving. Love to all. Harry

many Boers were killed we don't know.

According to last night's orders we are to have a standing camp here for two days but they may be altered inside the next few hours, we never know. We got ordered out this morning in an awful hurry but it turned out to be a false alarm.

This is the same lot of hills as we were in the time we got all the oranges but the

Soldier Boy

Boers have been here again since then and in consequence that kind of fruit is scarce though lemons are still to be found in large quantities and large size too for I never saw lemons in NZ either for size or flavour.

Yesterday after we got into camp we were visited by a very heavy thunder storm. Not the first but by far the worst we have experienced. Without tents or cover of any kind you can imagine what an African thunderstorm means to us chaps. The lightning is simply grand. It seems to set fire to everything and comes out of the clouds, which seem literally to lay on the ground, in long forked tongues of blue and yellow flame and strike with a beautiful zig-zag for the ground, and the thunder which follows instantly on the flash shames anything we ever heard in the Colony. It just goes bang like forty thousand fifteen pounders and one of them doesn't go off in a whisper.

What troubled us most was the rain and hail that it brought. It just poured and in 10 minutes the camp, which was on a slope, was a running sheet of water and hailstones. You can fancy the rest. Wet saddles, wet men and tired ones, wet blankets and soaked biscuits. We didn't enjoy it; but made as merry as we could under the circumstances. The worst part is making down a bunk with wet blankets on a mattress of mud, but I slept like a top and dreamed as sweet as a child in spite of it all, but I guess it isn't very healthy doing things that way. Today we are all drying our clobber. I would like you women folk to have one peep at my sleeping gear. You'd be laid up with the DTs for a fortnight. Coats and blankets stiff with mud where they are dry and where they are not, well wet with it, but the nights are not quite so cold now.

It is easy to see that the wet season is coming on for a while back we never saw a cloud for weeks at once, and now we see some nearly every day. Anyone misses the clouds just at first but we soon got used to it. It's that what makes the days so hot. See us going out in the morning with great coats on and with out backs rounded up like frogs but before ten o'clock our bandoliers are next our shirts and our sleeves are up while we grumble at the sweltering heat.

Out in the veldt there is nothing between earth and sky and that makes it seem more dreary and hot than it really is. I don't mind the heat so much as yet though it is early to talk that way but the nights are a severe change in a very short time. I expect we will have tents served out to us before the rainy season fairly sets in. I hope so for it is not a nice thing to lay and sleep with rain drops as big as sparrow's eggs splashing round your ears for the roof of Mrs Starlight's boarding house does not

This illustration gives a clear indication of the kind of landscape in which the New Zealand soldiers found themselves for much of their time in South Africa. (COURTESY HOCKEN LIBRARY, DUNEDIN)

stop water. The night we were in Vereeniging we had a lot of the Tommies from the Yorkshire and West Kent regiments over at our camp and round the fire we had quite a vocal entertainment.

I do wish you folk in NZ could see one of these active service concerns though I'll admit the programme would perhaps require to be slightly more selected. It's

Soldier Boy

very amusing to hear the Tommies, speaking all in the same dialect, calling on each other for a song or recitation as the case might be. One will sit down near the fire and say "I'm goin to be cheermun." Then another will says "No you don't, you aint ad enough heducation, that's my place." After a few more witty sallies from both parties and No 1 declares that he "aint a goin to shift," No 2 will come out with some such speech as: "Augh well to save further trouble hand bloodshed ye can bide there but see and do your dooty and hold your blitherin tongue." So it is settled and the "Cheerman" has much pleasure etc in calling on Private Barry of the Royal West Kent for a song. "I a'nt a goen to sing for you nor your likes so thar. I cant sing any how and you knows it but arter you a callen on me if I could I oudn't". Such is a Tommy concert.

One thing is very sure to be noticed if you wait for the finish and that is the way they all spring to attention when God save the King is struck up, this needless to say always forms the finish of these affairs out here. These Tommies are the best natured fellows on earth I'm sure. The evening we went into depot we were talking to one and of course told him how we had been faring on the column for rations. About an hour later over he comes to my mate and myself with a couple of pounds of bacon and two candles besides a lump of chocolate. He excused his generosity by saying that he had been on the veldt himself. What he gave us may not sound much to you but out here it is a lot and when you come to consider that he had to go without that much himself, for he gave us that out of his own private rations, it is that much better still.

The spirit in which it was given pleased us as much as the gift itself and that was not a little. The next morning he was over with a slice of steak for us before we were out of bed and the same night he gave us a lot of jam. Although their language is far from the best they are fine fellows and the way they think of each other and help in anything that is going would set an example to many people who go to church.

I saw one fellow do what I thought was a very thoughtful act one morning. It was only a little thing but it will do as an example of what I was just speaking. Some of us chaps and some Tommies had been on outpost duty all night and in the morning a heavy fog came on. When it is foggy the night posts do not come in at daylight, and not only that for more men are sent out from camp to reinforce the ones already there in case of a rush. Well, some more Tommies came out to help us, and one of them goes up to another one who had been on duty all night and says. "You looks as though you been dyen for a smoke old pal. I thought on you out here. I couldn't find your tobacco so I brought out a bit extra of mine like." A little thing like that shows how they think of each other. Poor chaps the veldt is plastered with the graves of others just as good as themselves. A hundred here, one there and a score somewhere else many with nothing but stones to mark the spot in a good many cases.

Really, any one does not need to have too tender a heart out here. It's very sad sometimes to see the rough and hurried care some living man has bestowed on his dead comrades. One grave I remember well had a rough cross worked in bits of rock on the top of it and a bit of biscuit box with a few lines on it in pencil. In memory of so and so of the Devons. Killed in action on such and such a day 1901. "God is love." All this in a rough scrawl but it tells its own tale. The one who did it evidently had as good a heart as the rest of the Tommies but like them too his bible was not as familiar to him as his drill book or he may have struck upon a text which would have better applied to the case. I suppose he thought that there should have been a text of some kind and maybe the one he so hurriedly scrawled in pencil was the only one he knew. I must pull up now or you will think I have got the floor properly.

But before I stop I must thank you for the full account of Jessie's illness and improvement you gave me. Miles away from everyone and everything that makes life worth living you do not know what such news as yours meant, to even such a thoughtless and heartless joker as I am reckoned to be. I thank you ever so much for leaving your letter stand over until you got back from town and could give me the very latest news about her. After coming away out here as I did you may think that thanks from me is an empty and worthless thing. Think as you may like, if I live to get back you may find that I don't belong entirely to Satan after all, and if I don't I guess what you think won't bother me for I'm used to sleeping on the ground now.

Write when you can and give me all that is worth giving and don't think too hard of that "Jumping Jackass" of a brother of yours who went away to the war. Remember me to Mrs Cromie and Alice and the Carlys girls when you get the chance and as I said just now, Write soon to your Aff Bro.

Harry

Paarde Kop

Sunday September 8th 1901

My Dear Sister

Not knowing when I will get another chance to write to you I am going to get another letter under way now. I wrote a big letter to Mother a day or two ago from Meyerton and sent it away with one for Louis and Percy too. I hope it will land safely in Cust before you get this.

You will no doubt wonder how it is that we are away down here when we were up there such a short time ago. Needless to say we did not treck down but were fetched in the train. We had a standing camp at Meyerton for two days and then orders suddenly came to treck down to Vereeniging and entrain there. At three o'clock on Thursday morning we were bundled out and a quarter to five we were off. Vereeniging is only about 9 miles south of the place we were at so it did not take us long to get down there and then start the business of entraining.

At Elandsfontein we stopped for half an hour and I assure you that the time was not wasted for there is a soldiers home there where you can get four cups of coffee and eight buns for a shilling and naturally we had a big splash. How welcome those prices were you will know when I tell you that at Vereeniging we had to pay 1/- for a cup of coffee and one bun, 3/6 for an ordinary dinner, 1/- for a sandwich, and the same for a bottle of lemonade.

At 4am yesterday morning we arrived here and then came the reverse of No. 1 operation. That of unloading. This we were at all day and last night it was like heaven to be allowed to turn into blankets once again after two nights practically without sleep. Such is warfare.

This place is forty miles south of Standerton I believe but I wouldn't be sure about that. We are told that there is tough work in front of us and that might be for we are after Botha if reports are true. All hands are expecting great things by the 15th of this month but I think most of the Boers now on the field are too pig-headed to give in but time will tell. If they don't give in there is no doubt that what fighting there is after that date will be desperate and the Lord help such of us as may fall into their hands for they will show very little mercy but if they make a stand we will eat them alive.

For those of us who get back there will be many pleasant things in store. It will be pleasant to ride in a tram without fear of being blown into the air by dynamite, to be able to go out without a rifle and bandoliers, to be able to undress every night and sleep without stones sticking in their ribs, to have as much before them at mealtimes as they can eat and that not bully beef or biscuits, to be able to sleep in every morning until six o'clock and then to be called to breakfast not ordered out on an empty stomach after Boers, to have tea with sugar in it and not more than half an ounce of mud per pint, and lastly but not least to be able to please themselves a little and not be part of a machine.

It's a great life out here. It's very strange but I never was on such short commons in my life before and I never put up with so many hardships in the way of loss of sleep and cold sleeping but as to health I could not be better. I enjoy every meal and you can tell Mother that I follow my Grandfather's rule and always knock off eating when I could eat a bit more (a good bit more sometimes, reason obvious).

I don't like looking forward to the rainy season and it's coming now very shortly. The fever is putting in an appearance now, one of our chaps has it very bad. He is away in the hospital. The doctors over here say the water swarms with it and when the hot weather gets fairly here sometimes one good drink is enough to give one a dose. I hang off water in consequence, though some fellows say it's rot and drink as much as they want. The fellow who has it now was one of that sort.

It's a great trial I know after marching hours in the heat and dust and dry as a wooden idol to refrain from drinking when one does come to water but it's worth the trying I think. It's all very well when a fellow is strong and well to say "Oh hang the fever. I'm going to drink when I want to," but when a fellow is on the broad of his back and raving like a lunatic it's a very different tale and too late then.

I see by the returns that the fever and dysentery has killed over three times as many as have lost their lives in action. So I think that it is worthwhile taking a bit of trouble to keep clear of it. I don't wonder at disease getting such a hold on chaps out here for when stations go short a fellow has no chance to combat anything in the way of ailments.

On our first Ermelo treck, which I told you about in my second letter from Standerton, it was something cruel. We took a lot of prisoners and rations ran

Soldier Boy

short. I may just mention here that prisoners get full rations and there were
we going hungry while our enemies were getting our shares. Reckon that was
carrying out scripture but it was due to no religious tendency of our own.

Well we used to get 2 biscuits a day there and two oz's of jam. More than once
hunger compelled me to eat all mine as soon as I got it and go without all day. But
that is partly wandering from the subject I was talking about, disease. Well as I
have just shown you we were nearly starved and many's a time we used to come
across a sheep on the march and as soon as we got into camp kill it, cut out the
biggest pieces of meat and fling them into the fire. After it was about hot right
through and the outside black it would be taken out and devoured without bread
(biscuit I should say) or salt, or pepper. This is the honest truth Lot and no stretch
for I was as bad as anyone. I've seen fellows chewing at the meat with the blood
running down their chins and that same meat not an hour before was running
about the veldt.

This is not very nice reading I know, and it was not very nice eating either but
I am stating plain facts. Is it any wonder that on that treck heaps of fellows were
laid up with dysentery.

Now I am going to say something about a different subject and that is the Field
Hospital Nurses. When I was in NZ I used to hear various stories about these
ladies; some of which did not do them much credit, but I tell you this, don't you
believe any of them that you may hear for the average nurse out here is one of the
best mortals that God has placed on this sinful earth. You'll say that I haven't been
in hospital and so don't know, but don't I that's all. I'm not blind and I seen plenty
who have been in there and know, besides nurses that I have seen myself. Folks
say that she is hardened but that's not so. True, she can talk about shattered limbs
and men killed by shells, as easily as you would speak about the latest fashions
but just let her come in contact with suffering and see then if she is hardened. It's
a touch here and a touch there and a little turn of a pillow somewhere else, just
exactly where and when it is needed, and whatever is wanted is always there. Some
men are pretty good at looking after fellows who are wounded but by jingo it takes
one of these nurses to square things up. There's no "Oh poor fellow where are you
hit. Are you in much pain. What can I do for you," about these. It's a moment's
glance then they know all about it and the rest comes like magic. They have
nothing to gain by staying out here; all the novelty is worn off long ago but they

Trooper Harry Gilbert, seen here in full regalia, probably posed for this studio photograph before setting off for South Africa in April 1901 with the 7th Canterbury Mounted Rifles.
(*Gilbert Family Collection*)

stay for the sake of the suffering pure and simple and the lowest Tommy is not too forgetful to salute one of them when they come his way and everywhere their red cross is treated with a respect bordering on reverence which it and its bearer so richly deserve.

I'm going to stop now
so Au Revoir

Write soon and often to a wandering and Dirty Rascal.

Natal, Newcastle
September 23rd 1901

My Dear Father

I am going to try and scribble you a few lines to let you know a little more about our doings over here. I got a letter to you and Mother well under way at Charleston but we got orders to entrain there in such a deuce of a hurry that I had to top it off and post it without getting to a finish.

I'm a bit of a toff in my way today for I have a biscuit tin for a desk and a swag to sit on and as the weather is just perfect today I'm enjoying myself immense, as far as it is possible to do that over here. I told you about entraining from Vereeniging to Paarde Kop and also about our trecking over the mountains of Zulu and Swaziland so I need not go into that again. We had a miserable time of it – thunder and rain nearly all the time so duckings and wet bivouacs were the order of the day. We also had another bad time coming down from Charlestown to here for it rained all the time and as per usual we were perched on top of wagons and in open trucks where we got the full benefit of the storm and it was awfully cold too but today is a perfect day so we will try and forget that we were ever wet and we have got all our blankets dry too for which we are very thankful.

We made a night march from here on Saturday night at five o'clock and camped sometime pretty late away out towards Utretcht but when Sunday Morn broke we got orders to come back at once so we immediately reversed the cogs and now here we are again. It's a busy time here now I assure you for if all accounts are true they have Botha about beggared away out in the south-east. Of course it may not be correct but we hear that there are five columns around him and six sections of artillery so if that is so Croje and Paardeberg will be played over again, at any rate they have been hurrying troops and guns down the line at top speed for the last 24 hours. Train after train going at top speed and loaded with horses, guns, men, fodder and war material. I hear that we are to entrain again for Ladysmith and I expect it is true, if it is we will see service under French before long. For the honour of the regiment I would like the 7th New Zealanders to have a fist in the capture of Botha.

There was a train blown sky high the other night this side of Paarde Kop but we haven't heard about the injuries yet. We are having a very busy time and precious little sleep so you will believe me when I say that we are always more or less sleepy. We got down here the other night about half past nine, in the rain and darkness, but wet and cold as we were they ran a searchlight up in front of us and we had to unload everything in the mud. It was a great time and after it was all over we were allowed as a favour to sleep on the stones under a veranda but we were up and away again at daylight.

Here comes two more trains loaded with troops and making south at top. By Jove there must be something going on and I hope we get sent down and have a chance. They don't do things by halves out here in the fighting line and if Botha is really surrounded and won't give in, they will blow him and his brother Jackies to Kingdom come, poor beggars.

I guess you will be about sick of my letters, full as they are of accounts of wet and hunger and this time I must try and leave such subjects strictly alone and try and give you something different and take the risks about it being interesting. Whatever I fill up with you will have to excuse pencil, and scribble, for I have to go at top because it's only at odd times a fellow gets the chance to write and time is precious.

By jingoes there's some awful lies told in letters from here and to us who are on the ground and read them in the papers they look very ridiculous. For instance we were reading a letter yesterday from a trooper, or a Sergt I should say who was at Standerton. Among other things he said that Standerton was on the Natal border and from where he was writing he could see Laings Nek and Majuba. This is only one statement out of many but for downright untruth it put all the others into the shade. As a matter of fact the town mentioned is about eighty miles above the border and the nature of the country makes it just as possible to see Hokitika from Oxford as to see either Laings Neck or Majuba either from there. What fellows can see in sending home such rot I don't know more especially when the credulity of its readers makes it run a serious risk of getting into papers. Personally I can generally find enough truth to talk about without troubling my imagination by trying to think out lies, but all people are not alike in that way. I am posting a letter to Tom Jones this mail and in it I have put a rough plan of the place where we had a stand up go with De La Reys men at Vet Kop out Lyndique Drift way and I have asked him to let you have a look at it as it might interest you to see the lay of the country where the Boers made their stand against our Column.

If the weather would only keep like it is now we would not be so bad off but before many hours are over it will be thundering again in all probability and if not it will be cold enough to freeze anyone. It's a very strange climate out here and I often think that if you were living in it, for the first three months you would have a lively and busy time studying the various changes of the weather for it is never to be depended on now that the season has changed. It's a fine winter though, no rain at all and though it is terribly cold at night you can kick dust up at any time, but that is over now worse luck in a good many ways.

I wrote a letter to Louis the other day and told you, or him I should say about a little scene we had between one of our scouts, a QIB (Queensland Imperial Bushmen), and Colonel White. He was tried by Court martial and sentenced to a year's hard labour and the Queensland portion of our column were having their spite out on "Old Harry" as the Col is called by letting off their rifles and revolvers at intervals all that day, a thing which particularly displeases him , but which he had too much common sense to protest against or kick up a fuss about, for there are many men in the ranks of the colonials who would just as soon put a bullet into him as they would a Boer for this is active service and no one can see where bullets come from but we hope it won't come to that. He has an awful "set" on the Colonials at any rate. There's not discipline and red tape enough among them to please his mind and they won't obey his orders when he comes any of his games. He issued special orders that none of us were to carry wood into camp on our horses, so we carry it up to the camp boundaries on them and then get off and carry it into the camp on our shoulders, a matter of a chain or two. When he saw us at that he cursed us up hill and down dale but did not change the order.

At Charlestown the other day he issued orders that no one was to go into town but we had no sooner camped than off goes a lot of fellows for bread. When they came back he walked up to one chap who was rejoicing over three or four loaves and vented a torrent of curses and suchlike on his head.

"I can't make you colonials out atall," he raved. "Here I issue orders and they are no sooner out than you go straight and disobey them. If I give imperial men orders they are obeyed but you colonials don't care for orders or anything else. D--- you all I say."

Our chap saluted and told him straight that we had never been used to being absolutely controlled by the will of others and liked to please ourselves without being hampered with a lot of bunkum at every turn, but nevertheless he was imprisoned for three days and fined 15 shillings.

For little things like this we all heartily dislike "Molly White" or "Old Harry" as he is styled in the lines. Nearly all the Imperial officers are the same. Brave as lions but entirely eaten up with red tape and drill book nonsense which is absolutely no use out here. The other day I was selected to go orderly galloper to a Major of the Royal West Kent Regiment and when I rode up and reported myself, "Ah very good" was all I got beside a look which seemed to say "You are a dirty rascal." Truly I was a picture, mud up to the neck and wet into the bargain but I plumed myself that I could sit a horse across country with him so I fell back a couple of horse lengths and started to whistle and sing in colonial fashion. He looked round mighty black and I saw the Tommies behind pointing to me and doing a smile. But I said to myself "Alright old chap if you want to make me shut up you can say so, looks won't do it." However he said nothing and presently it was: "Orderlah, gallop down and tell those companies on the right to wheel round to the left and extend in the reah of the convoy." I saw him smile and look at me as much as to say "That'll puzzle you," and truly the country was mighty rough but in went my spurs and taking him at his word off I went at a rattling gallop over some hills and holes, down a gully and up the other side jumping a stream as I went for his confident smile made me wild. I delivered his orders then rode back. For sheer spite I broke the rule and galloped bang up to him and pulled my horse on his beam ends and said "That's done sir." "Ah" says he, "Good, very good," and then I dropped to the rear again.

Next time it was "Ride up and tell those chaps on the left they need not go ovah that kopje, they can go round it," without the smile this time. I did that and came jogging back whistling "Yankee Doodle". Then all his reserve and "hauh hauh" style vanished and he started to talk to me as right as a man could be. So it happened, for the rest of the day's treck we were asking questions about NZ and England alternately and when he laid drill book bunkum aside he was a thorough gentleman. There was no more "Orderlah do this, or go thereah," after that it was "Take a jog up and tell them this or that" without the drawl. He knew Andover and wanted to know a lot about NZ and the way things were worked over there, so when night came we parted quite friendly.

Colonials can't put up with the air of superiority which some of these Imperial men assume, but to their credit be it said that they never disobey an order or even question it when the bullets are flying and though I may say it myself it would be

Soldier Boy

SOUTH AFRICA
1901-02
BOER WAR

Like so many soldiers serving during a time of
war, Harry had plenty of time on his hands and
he used much of it to carve the stock of his Long
Tom .303 rifle. (*Gilbert Family Collection*)

Soldier Boy

hard to find a lot of men to beat them when there's a cross country gallop after Boers in the wind. Taken all round they are full of dash and daring. Even Old Harry admits that though I daresay it's against his will. Though it truly is a very rousing thing to sweep forward at a gallop with your rifle loaded and at the "Advance".

Its marvellous how bullets miss you. They go through hats, waterbottles, coat-sleeves and everywhere but very seldom hit a man. A fellow that does get hit is looked upon as unlucky. Also it's not a stretch to say that the guns put shells over our heads – they do and sometimes you think your head is blown off.

I hope that I haven't wearied you with my rubbish but if I have take it like the man did the kick from the donkey and burn it out of your sight.

I must stop now, will put more if I get the chance.

Adieu, Your Aff Son
Harry

My Dear Mother, Later . . .

Quite in the usual run of things I get knocked off writing in an awful hurry and as I have this much space to fill I thought that I would just put in a line or two for you so that you would see that I don't forget that I have a Mother as well as a Father. I have pretty well exhausted my stock of news and what I have written is probably of such a nature that it will sadden rather than interest you, but you know Mother it's war out here and as for homely everyday news there is absolutely none of it.

You must not worry about me and my surroundings, I'm alright and in the best of health yet and I hope to continue so. I don't seem to think the bullet is moulded that is to kill me for already I have had a lot to choose from and am still without a scratch. I've had a few upsets off my horse of course, but everybody gets them.

You must excuse this scribble as I'm in a great hurry to finish. We have heard that we are not to entrain tonight so I am going to try and have a big night's rest. By the time I have served my twelve months I won't know how to write at a desk or table again and you'll see me cruising around for a bit of tin or board to serve in their place.

It's getting near teatime now and I am sure you will excuse me from writing

After coming under fire under a number of occasions, Trooper Harry Gilbert and his companions quickly learned to be wary of approaching Boer farm houses and outbuildings such as these on the African veld. (PHOTO COURTESY HOCKEN LIBRARY, DUNEDIN)

more seeing that that is so. Remember me to good old Mrs Cromie and to all who may ask for me but I expect they are not many. "Thus let me live unseen unknown" etc. I really can't write any more just now. I'll wait until I get another mail from NZ. In the meantime don't forget me and keep the letters going to

Yours with Love
Harry

I don't know how much you have to pay on the letters I send without stamps. I hope it isn't much or you will bless me and my writings but I can't get stamps so what am I to do. I must post this now for out here as I told Louis "Tempus Fugit".

So once again
Au Revoir

Pandawana
October 6th 1901

Dear Father

As we are keeping a standing camp we are inlying squadron today and there being so far very little doing I am going to write a few lines to you. I have sad news to tell this time. I hope you won't worry too much about it but you will see it in the papers before this is on the water so the news won't be a surprise to you.

Billy Smith and Sergt Dungan both of Canty Squadron and likewise both of my troop were killed yesterday morning on Gellak Hill just a little over from here.

We had a terrible time of it while it lasted and I am thankful that I am spared to tell the tale. Our squadron was on what is called day outpost yesterday and immediately after daybreak we split up into our respective troops and went out to take up position on a range of hills to the east of the camp. When we got out to the range we found that the hill which No 2 troop (mine) was to hold was already occupied by Boers who let us come close up and then sprang a great surprise on us by opening fire at close range. The Sergt was out in front and he must have been shot first at close range as none of us saw him fall. We got back to cover, handed over our horses and then crept back up the ridge in extended order. For a while the Boers raked the ridge with bullets and then their fire slackened. As soon as the lead ceased to come poor old Billy Smith did a very foolish thing. He's gone now poor fellow, but the truth must be told. He stood up on the ridge, and leaning on his rifle said that "he couldn't see any bloomen Boers". Of course they were only waiting for something of this sort, and he instantly fell mortally wounded. I'll never forget it for I was not more than six paces from him and the bullet went right through him and just missed me. At that moment we were ordered to retire and that was the hardest task of all, though there was nothing else left for us to do. It was impossible to get up to him for the bullets were hissing and to show yourself was certain death.

Another chap on the left of Billy and a little further up crawled down but could do nothing so away we had to go. It did bring Jim's death back vividly to my mind for Bill's breathing was just the same sound only worse.

We galloped back followed by the crack of the bullets and took cover behind a steep rocky face. Then the grand finished was played for our own artillerymen

Pandawana
October 6th 1901

Dear Father

As we are keeping a standing camp & we are inlying squadron today & there being so far very little doing I am going to write a few lines to you. I have sad news to tell this time & I hope you wont worry too much about it but you will see it in the papers before this on the water so the news wont be a surprise to you. Billy Smith & Sergt Dungan both of C? squadron & likewise both of my troop were killed yesterday morning on Telak Hill just a little over from here. We had a terrible time of it while it lasted & I am thankful that I am spared to tell the tale. Our squadron was on what is called day outpost yesterday & immediately after daybreak we split up into our respective troops & went out to take up positions on a range of hills to the east of the camp. When

(2)

we got out to the range we found that the hill which No 2 troop (mine) was to hold was already occupied by Boers who let us come close up & then sprang a great surprise on us by opening fire at close Range. The Sergt was in front & he must have been shot first at close range, as none of us saw him fall. We got back to cover handed over our horses & then crept back up the ridge in extended order. For a while the Boers raked the ridge with bullets & then their fire slackened. As soon as the lead ceased to come poor old Billy Smith did a very foolish thing. He's gone now poor fellow but the truth must be told. He stood up on the ridge & leaning on his rifle said that he couldn't see any bloomen Boers. Of course they were only waiting for something of this sort, & he instantly fell mortally wounded. I'll never forget it for I was not more than six paces from him & the bullet went right through him & just missed me. At that moment we were ordered to retire

took us for Boers and turned their artillery on to us. You have probably seen the 6 pound Nordenfelt guns that the [A letter is given here, possibly D, G or C] Battery have in ChCh and that being so you can imagine what it is like to stand up to guns that throw a shell which is 2 times heavier than the ones they fire. They aimed beautifully too for the first shell landed fairly amongst us. It did not occur to us that it was done on purpose and I said to my mate "that was a lucky escape chappy; the gunners have made a bloomer this time for that one is about half a mile short." I just turned round and with a hiss and scream another burst closer than the other.

To say that we were in a fix gives no idea of the thing at all. We knew that to go back over the ridge would bring dozens of Boer's bullets at us while it would make the gunners redouble their efforts from the other side. Talk about being between the Devil and the deep sea, that wasn't a patch on it.

We have been praised for our pluck since but we didn't think it was bravery but sheer desperation that made us quit the rock and advance towards those fire spitting cannon. When we did this they ceased to fire for Boers never advance towards big guns and they had two trained on us and firing at top. As soon as they saw who we were things were speedily changed. Three doctors and two ambulance wagons galloped up to us from the column (they had stood off and shelled us from about 1 miles). It was a perfect miracle but not a man was hit, it's marvellous, for all the shells landed inside an area of a few square chains and inside that area we were. I don't want to face big guns again.

When you feel the wind of them and get a dirty face from the dust thrown up by their explosions they are going close enough. The Sergt Major of the artillery apologised to us, thanked God when he found out that no one was hurt while one of the gunners scratched his head and said "I'd a cussed myself to my dyen day if we'd a passed some on you out for I'm one of the chaps as was trainen the bloomen guns." We congratulated him on his skills and then the matter dropped.

Big guns don't give you the awful suspense that a pom pom gun does because they only send one shell at a time and as it travels quicker than the sound you can't hear it coming. It's a scream and a deafening crash and a flash of yellow fire and it's over until next time. With a pom pom on the other hand you first hear the pom pom pom pom pom of the gun and then follows a very trying two or three seconds until the scream of the string of shells is heard. With a big shell if it misses you, you are safe until another one comes which is a little time, but with a pom pom if one misses you, you know perfectly well that the next one might not and if they send (as they sometimes do) a string of 25 at one go the time from the landing of the first to the bursting of the last is certainly not pleasantly spent for they go here, there and everywhere.

But enough of this for I don't want to face either any oftener than can be helped much less our own men.

More sad news has just come in for at 3 o'clock this morning some of our scouts went out and one Queenslander was shot dead and two 7th NZ's wounded. One is Billy Rutherford who was wounded before in the arm at Lyndique Drift (shot through the leg this time) and the other is W Campbell. We wonder whose turn it will be next.

We are keeping a standing camp here and we are playing into someone else's hand or else we would not stop here. We know for certain that the British columns are close handy. After I left W Smith on the hill I never saw him again for both he and Dungan were taken into camp and buried very soon after while I was away until night with an outpost.

This portion of the letter ends abruptly here, with just three lines completed on the last page. The letter is continued six days later, in what is obviously a rather shaky hand.

Field Hospital, Vryheid October 12th

I'm just going to try and finish this sheet. You will be surprised to see me in a hospital but the day I started this I had to cave in with Dutch Measles [sic] and a dash of fever thrown in. For three days I was mighty bad and hung on but at last I was forced to go under. Since then I have been fed on pills and milk and water and naturally I don't feel very fit now.

I have written a line to Jessie and am just writing this to you in case things go wrong which I hope they won't. Will write a letter to Mother when I get stronger. All of us sick came in here by bullock convoy yesterday. Had another big go with Botha 23 casualties in all (6 more NZ'rs). Must stop now for I'm "weary". Hoping to send more soon.

I am Aff Son
Harry

October 13th

Am doing good O. Will write again when I'm just a bit more "fit" like. Don't fret cause I don't.

Harry

Jammed into the tiny space between the end of the first letter and the start of the second is this note of October 13th.

Soldier Boy

Field Hospital SA
Vryheid Oct 18ᵗʰ 1901

*Written to his sister in
tiny writing, this letter in
indelible pencil required
the aid of a magnifying
glass to transcribe it.*

Dear Lottie

I'm taking a new departure this time in the way of crowding because I am fairly on "bedrock" and have got down to my last sheet of notepaper. In fact I am absolutely in a bad way stranded in here without a steever. As this is an out of the way place without a hope of getting any I mustn't complain for I might be in a far worse fix. You people will be thinking that I have completely forgotten you or that I have been snuffed out or something of the kind for I see by my diary that it is three weeks past since I posted my last in Newcastle. But I can't help it really for we have been trecking after Botha and having supplies sent out to us and not going into towns for them ourselves so you see that to post letters was impossible.

I know very well you will be worrying or at least I am "cocky" enough to think that you will be but it can't be helped. The worst of it is that I don't know when I will be able to get this away either, it may be soon or it may be a month.

We know absolutely nothing here. We don't know where our column is or how they are faring so I can give you no column news this time. I would have been with them now if I hadn't got tripped up with these confounded measles. However, I was in the thick of it while the fighting was on and Botha sneaked through the night I came in so I may not have missed much. Of course it is much easier for us here than with the column but still I want to get back to the "boys" out on the veldt taking my share.

We hear rumours, and are living in hopes of being sent down to Dundee (two days treck). That at any rate is a railway town and we will be able to get some clothes there if nothing else and goodness knows we need them. You will of course understand that I am not alone, far from it, for one is never alone in anything out here and particularly if it's in misfortune. I am with a lot more chaps who are in the same boat as myself, without money and only what clothes they stand in. This with diverse other little irregularities is the reward of those who put in their time "Fighting for the dear old colonies" but I'm still being fed and my pay is being earned just the same so here's to Merry

England and I don't care if the cat goes to the pound. Do you? What annoys us most of all is that we measle cases are isolated and must not go out of a certain boundary (a mighty small one) but we hope this bit of bunkum will soon be done away with.

As I said before, this little place is fairly out of the world and they are, or seem to be, short of everything. For instance at breakfast time, when they have porridge, they serve up four men's allowance in a tin bowl, sugared, and ready for the palate and with one spoon. We asked the orderly yesterday if he was feeding hogs and so far we have got no satisfactory reply. Maybe he is studying our characters before he makes answer.

I may as well tell you here that we are all doing well and are on full rations again so it's only a question of time before we are right as a fiddle again. It would have been better for me if I had given in sooner, but there are such a lot of fellows who jump at a chance of going "sick" to miss the bullets, that unless it is really something serious a chap who goes to the doctor is laughed at in the lines and the fellows say (and rightly in some cases) that he is suffering from an attack of "Mauseritis" "Pom Pom fever" or "Bulletaria". Consequently I hung out. The day we had the scrap I was horrible crook and that night I was worse but I made my bunk down against an anthill and put in a night of fitful naps interspersed with studies of astronomy. Next day we were inlying squadron and in the morning I was able to be about and rest my aching bones, but in the afternoon the Jackies must needs go and attack our outposts and we were ordered out.

By this time the measles were out all over me and I was like a piece of beef but I got my bandolier on and my rifle but that was all for I'm beggared if I could get into the saddle. I had to stay behind and had the pleasure of seeing another chap ride off to do battle on my horse.

Over to the ambulance I goes, sees the doctor who, with an "Oh my Lord" ordered me to bed at once in a hospital tent with some more unfortunates. Then comes a course of pills and milk, up goes my temperature to the big figures over the 100, down comes my strength and "What ho she bumps" HGG's got the fever and Dutch Measles. "Don't give him anything but milk." Oh Lor, how bad did I feel eh, a steam hammer in my head and an ache wherever an ache was possible, bumped along in the red cross wagons all day and glowing like a coal all night. Just what I call Kapai.

At last all of us sick and wounded got sent into here and we are all going to be fighting again soon "gin we're spared".

I think I mentioned in Dad's (which isn't posted yet) that the day of the big "go" our side had 28 casualties. Since we left Buffalo Bridge we have been working in conjunction with another column and they lost pretty badly that day. The Western Australians had some hit and the 18th and 19th Hussars had something like eight killed and as many wounded while our column had six Nz'rs wounded. During the few days we were there (at Pandawana) both of our columns had about 32 men killed and wounded. Eight of our 7th were wounded and two killed. The Boers lost something under 150 as our big gun fire was just something terrible. Over 30 graves were found and many of them were double while they had a deuce of a lot wounded.

What has transpired since I don't know but I'm hoping to be with the column again soon wherever they are got to.

I intended to fill this sheet to Mother but with ordinary writing I concluded that I could get nothing in and as she couldn't read this sort of stuff I am sending it to you so you must share the news with her, what there is.

Before we left Newcastle we were given a concert by the garrison and the Royal Dublin Fusiliers' band. It was a treat which we all very much enjoyed I can tell you.

It seemed quite the thing to hear "Last Rose of Summer" and "The Girl I Left Behind Me" ringing out on the brass to the deep boom of a drum. These affairs given out here on active service always have a go and a freedom about them that is never seen under ordinary circumstances and as everybody knows that he will have the rifles cracking around him before he hears the like again they are always thoroughly enjoyed and made the most of.

On our way out we trecked through Utrecht. That is a very pretty little township, not very big but very nicely arranged and it looks very nice. All these Dutch places look very nice and they always have a very presentable church in the centre for they seem to have been a great church-going people. At this place there is also a nicely laid off race course and grandstand.

It's just a fortnight ago today that poor old Billy Smith and our Sergt got killed on Gelak Hill. I told Dad all about it so I need not go into it again. I'll never forget it though, for I was nearly pipped on the same hill myself. They were buried side

Heroic acts were regularly reported — and illustrated — in the newspaper coverage back home. In this example New Zealand soldiers are depicted saving their Maxim machine gun after a rout by Boer soldiers. (Photo courtesy Hocken Library, Dunedin)

Soldier Boy

by side under some wattle trees. They were buried the same afternoon as they were killed and as I was on day outpost I never saw either of them after they were shot. I was sorry for even with rough old Billy there may have been someone who would have liked a piece of his hair but I couldn't work it. Poor old Bill he went out with us that morning in great spirits. Full of Barrack and jokes and he had a leg and shoulder of mutton tied together and slung across his saddle for, as he said, he was going to make a fire and have a "bloomen good feed through the day". But wasn't to be.

Up the hill we went and a few minutes after it was "Crack, Whizz, Phut" and Billy was moaning his life out on the veldt in front of me. Talk about bullets they did bung them in, but it's over now. I am sending you a few of the leaves and a piece of bark from the tree that waves over them. Look after them for me.

In Dad's last letter to me, while speaking of the dangers and hardships of life out here he said that he guessed I wished that I had never saw South Africa and I suppose he was only voicing the opinions of all of you. Well let me tell you all that if I had been going to wish that, I would have stayed in NZ while I was there. I don't think that you credit me with having much sense or reason or you wouldn't think that I would wish myself out of it. I didn't come out here expecting to get fed on sponge roll. I'll admit that there are many hardships which I didn't reckon on and also that bully beef and biscuits or an empty stomach is nothing near the same as it used to appear down in the kitchen there when I had plenty to eat and a warm fire to sit over but in spite of hunger and sleeplessness, ragged clothes and dirt, and shells and bullets, I am quite willing to put in my twelve months out here and take my chances with the hundreds of others who are out here "wiping something off the slate". I think that I have just about got down as low as I can get now. I'll tell you my latest caper. I've got about three inches of hair on my head and there is a barber's shop just behind our "boundary". I must have my hair cut and I haven't got a red cent so whats to be done. I've sold a nigger an old, dirty and ragged shirt, for 1/-. Just fancy. After that I don't pretend you want to see me again, but I'm going to get my hair cut tomorrow. That will cost 6d and I must try and sneak away and get some note paper with the other few pence. Don't you reckon it's come to something with HHG. when it comes to that.

Writing this style is tiring work so I'll stop until tomorrow so Au Revoir.

October 21ˢᵗ and still in Vryheid

I'm going to try and finish this now although today as you will see by the date is not the "tomorrow" I spoke of when I left off. Howsomever, better late than never. There is still not a scrap of news except that they are trying to get us sent down to Dundee to get on the track of our column. We hope it's true.

I have just written a letter to Mother and as I have not been able to post Dad, I am going to open it and send them all together. I hope to be able to get them away soon or else you will be thinking that I have "gone up" as the Tommies say.

There is a lot of Cameron or Seaforth Highlanders knocking about today as there must be a column in. I saw the far famed "Fighting Fifth" Northumberland Fusiliers on the railway and they looked a brawny and suntanned lot. Truly they looked like fighters.

I have had never a word from any of those brothers of mine excepting Louis. They seem to have forgotten my existence. I didn't expect letters from Bill or Jack, I guess they only think I'm fit for "Cannon Meat", but I thought Joe and Fred might write. I suppose Joe is happy go lucky and doesn't worry his head about me or anyone else and Fred is too much taken up with a certain brown eyed maiden to bother with a far off trooper. However good luck to him. He is the best man in the Gilbert family.

I'm going to stop now. Remember me to Mrs Cromie and write again soon to

Harry

This last page is turned sideways, and in an expansive hand Harry has scrawled at right-angles to the main text of his letter the last few words.

Soldier Boy appears as a running header.

Field Hospital, Vryheid

October 21ˢᵗ 1901

Mr Dear Mother

I am going to try and fill this sheet to you and put it in along with the rest which I am afraid will be sadly out of date by the time it reaches NZ. I have no news to tell.

As you will see by the others, letters I am stranded here in this out of the way and back country town about forty miles from a town and without information of any sort. No doubt you will all be greatly surprised to see me in the Hospital. I was surprised myself but it couldn't be helped. Ever since we captured those Boers out from Honningspruit the measles have been booming in our column for some of the prisoners had them and as a natural consequence we took them too. I thought that I had escaped as that is over two months ago and dozens of our fellows have had them since then but my turn came and I did just get a dose.

I have yourself and Dad to thank for one thing if nothing else and that is a good clear constitution which is a grand thing out here. Both the measles and fever have left me now without any troublesome after effects which are very noticeable on many others who have had the same thing. Of course I'm not terribly strong yet but that is coming. Three of us did a sneak out for a walk in the evening and we got a great surprise when after fifteen minutes steady strolling we were clean tired out and glad to get back.

This morning we have had our underclothing disinfected so our isolation will be over now. It's a bit funny though for all of us only have the one lot of clothes and at the present time we are poking about in trousers, boots, and tunics waiting for shorts, socks, pants etc to dry.

You will be able to imagine our condition or mine at least and it's the same with a good many more, when I tell you that I haven't set eyes on my kit since we arrived at the front nearly six months ago. It's laying [sic] with the rest in Pretoria. So you see I am here with my feet through my boots, legs through my trousers, and body very nearly through my shirt while laying in my kit is a pair of new boots, two pairs of trousers, heaps of underclothes, and in fact everything that I so badly want, but can't get at.

You will be worrying about news from me for I have gone a long time without being able to send a letter but I can't help it and even yet this may have to wait for another week before I can post if communications with this place are so bad.

Lottie will no doubt tell you about my little deal with the nigger. What do you think of that for your Soldier boy. I got had again too for I went as large as life in my questionable rigout and had my hair cut. A jail bird's clip, clean all over, and about five minutes work with the clippers and "A shilling please" says the barber so away goes my bob and no hope of getting any writing paper after that.

However, I was determined to get a letter written somehow so I barracked and at last got this sheet from our orderly, it was like drawing his teeth.

I hear that we are to be sent to Dundee, and from there by rail to join our column in a few days' time. I hope it's true for I'll soon be alright when I get astride the pig skin again.

Now Ta Ta "There'll come a Time Some Day" when I can get more paper.

Till then, Believe me, Your Loving Son

HGG

October 31ˢᵗ 1901

Dear Father

I am sending you one or two Boer photographs for a Christmas box. Not the most appropriate concerns for this time of the year, but certain, for the time being, more in my line than Christmas cards, and no doubt one at least (the photo which represents the seamy side of warfare as well as being a good photo of a scene, which, worse luck is very common in South Africa), will be very much in your line and will also furnish some work for your glass.

I have not time to write you any more now so heartily wishing you all a Very Merry Christmas and a Happy and Prosperous New Year, I remain, Your Aff Son.

HG Gilbert

Soldier Boy

*Harry included these two photographs and the one on page 84 in a letter to his father. Christian De Wet (above), the leader of the Boer fighters was a man of great charisma and a skilled tactician in the Boer commando style of fighting. He served in the Anglo-Boer War (First Boer War, 1880–81) and went on to become a prominent member of the Afrikaans Volksraad (Parliament) shortly before the outbreak of the Boer War in 1899. (G*ILBERT *F*AMILY *C*OLLECTION*)*

The Intombi cemetery at Ladysmith showing a number of fresh military and civilian graves, the inscriptions of which can be read with a magnifying glass. (GILBERT FAMILY COLLECTION)

Soldier Boy

Shown here are some of the captured munitions and other Boer War trophies taken by the New Zealanders including clips and ammunition belts of 7mm Mauser cartridges and a 7mm Mauser rifle, with which the Boers fought so successfully against the British and colonial forces. Also displayed are pieces of shrapnel, one-inch Pom Pom rounds, and a variety of artillery projectiles and shell cases. (GILBERT FAMILY COLLECTION)

November 8th 1901

Dear Sis

I'm just going to send you a few lines in a hurry. Some of us New Zealanders are to go down to Dundee tomorrow morning and as this is the last chance I will have to do a bit of writing in anything like comfort I am going to seize the opportunity and send you a few lines.

I am glad to be able to tell you that I am quite well again and am not a bit sorry for that same as sickness out here does not mean soft stationary beds and plenty of looking after. Not by any means.

Lately we have been having some terrible weather in the way of rain and thunder; both I may say in the most complete sense of the word. I never saw rain like it falls here. It's nothing less than liquid lumps of water falling like marbles. The thunder and lightning I think I have tried to describe before but no description of mine or anyone's I think could give an idea of what it is really like. When the clouds are low as they usually are you see a blinding glare of dancing yellow and blue fire which is followed instantly by a deafening crash like a battery of artillery going off but unlike that, as the crash is of a very lengthy duration. You seem to be in a sea of noise for the air fairly throbs with it and the ground trembles. Altogether it's most terrifying when you are mixed up in it, more especially at night when the blinding glare makes it as light as day for the time being and adds to the intensity of the inky darkness which immediately follows it.

The night before last I stood for a long time and watched it, wishing very much that you were here to see it too. It was grand (at a safe distance mind) to see, the blue chains tearing and dancing along the sky and making the clouds look as if they were all on fire.

I told you all about my hospital stay at Vryheid so I need not go over that ground again. It is not very far from there that the Prince Imp was killed and likewise it is no distance to where the Zulus were finally defeated by Mr John Bull.

The Zulus are a fine big and strong race (the men) and when in their war paint are not nice to look at for what with assagais and knobkerries they are armed to the teeth. I'd far and away face rifles and shells than a rushing mob of these fierce black imps.

This letter, along with its envelope, was written using a dip-pen and black indian ink. There is no postmark on the front of the envelope, but on the back it was stamped at four different post offices.

Soldier Boy

So help me bob I thought one old fellow was going to put an assagai through me one day. He had been droving sheep for our column and when we went into camp I went as usual and made mutton of one. The old chap could not see the right side of this at all. He thought that I was stealing it from "dah big baas" as they call the Colonel and as he was armed with "head bumper" and spear he wanted to settle it there and then and such a settlement as I had no desire to go shares in. My word how his hair did bristle and how he danced. I didn't feel very sure of my ground I tell you but putting on a bold front I told him mixed English and Pigeon Dutch that if he came too near me I'd "kick his liver out" (excuse). This sobered him down but if it had come to the doing of it I would have about as much chance of doing it as I would of flying and I would have had to trust to my legs to get me away from him and even there I fear I would have made a bad second.

When you write give me all the Xmas news and doings and your latest news of Jessie also, don't forget will you. Love to Mum Dad and all and just a bit extra like for yourself to go on with and believe me.

Your Loving Bro
Harry

The last three lines of this letter were scrawled hastily across the first page, at right-angles to the rest.

Once again A Merry Xmas and Happy N.Y to you all and Mrs Cromie as well. Don't forget me but don't get dumpy either but just rejoice in my absence and be glad I'll miss you all more than you will miss me I bet. Adieu.

Pandawana
November 18th 1901

My Dear Mother

As I was unable to send you anything of a letter from Vryheid this time I am going to start another one to you from here and do it at my usual "Diary" style, a bit now and another bit some other time so that by the time it is finished it will at any rate be something for you to read even if the quality of the same is not much.

To set yourself at rest about myself I will tell you right away that I am on duty again and just about as well as ever, for I seem to get better as quickly as I get bad once the worst is past. To tell you the truth I am not sorry to be free from the dysentery for it is a very troublesome and dangerous complaint out here and besides is very painful into the bargain.

Before I get fairly going with my epistle and skite I must confine myself to answering such questions and queries as are asked from time to time in your letters and which up to now I think I must have passed over in my replies. You ask about Walt Jones, Steve Whitta, C Cooper, Cassidy as well as Spencer and Jack Armstrong. Well, to put the last first I can tell you that Armstrong is in the hospital at Utrecht or was the last I heard of him, as he was taken very bad and had to be left there when the column came through to Newcastle. R Spencer is here with me now, he has been bad with the dysentery too but is about better now like myself. Cooper and Cassidy are as you know in the Sixth and so we never see them at all. I saw Dan six months ago at Standerton, but he was in with some more for remounts.

Some of the Sixth were in Newcastle when I came away, but they told me that both he and Charlie C were on their column (Plumer's) then. Steve Whitta was in the Newcastle base hospital when I was there but I did not see him as it is a bit out of the town. He got wind of it that I was in and he sent word for me to go and see him for he was likely to be going home, but I could not manage it. He is suffering from a weak heart I believe so in all probability he will see NZ before this does.

Why I have not mentioned them in my letters I don't know unless it is my innate selfishness which prompts me to write about nothing but myself and my doings.

You ask me do I ever see them. When we are all on column as we mostly have been up till now, of course I do for we are neighbours so to speak and it's only a

Pandawana
Nov 18th 190_

My Dear Mother

As I was unable to send you a
_____ of a letter from _____ this time, I am g__
to start another one to you from here & do __
__ any more "_____" style, a bit now & another
bit some other time so that by the time it __
finished it will at any rate be something
for you to read even if the quality of the
same is not much. To set yourself at res_
about myself I will tell you right away __
that I am on duty again & just about a_
well as ever, for I seem to get better an qui__
_ I get bad once the worst is past. To te__
you the truth I am not sorry to be free fr__
the dysentry for it is a very troublesome
dangerous ____plaint out here & besides ve_
painful into the bargain. Before I get far
____ with my epistle & skite I must confi__
myself to answering such questions & querri__
as are asked from time to time in you_
letters & which up to now I think I mu__
have passed over in my replies. You as__
about Walt Jones, Steve Whitta, C. Cooper
Cassidy, as well as Spencer & Jack Arm_

matter of a few yards into their lines at night and I used to have a yarn with both of them whenever I felt that way.

Our Column left Vryheid yesterday morning at 4AM, and for this purpose we were waked out of bed at 2AM. That is the usual reveille with us now and it is unheard of good luck if we get a chance to sleep in until 5 or later.

Dear Mother I smiled when I read in your letter, what you said about my writing under difficulties. I'll frankly own that it is too true, but how little you in NZ can realise what those "difficulties" really consist of. Wind and rain I am taking no count of, but really Mother if you could only but see some (some mind) of the situations and circumstances under which those letters of mine, which you honour me by calling "Interesting", are really produced, I honestly think that you would pardon me even were I to extend my time to three months between each letter.

However for your sake I am not going to do that while I am spared to move upon this Earth for I know how you all look to news from your headstrong soldier boy even if he does not come up to the standard that you would like him to. I don't think human nature is ever satisfied for I got seven letters at Vryheid the other day and even then I was not satisfied because I didn't get a line from Dad. Of course he never writes long letters, but he has a way of "condensing" his correspondence, and making much go into little; which, unfortunately his Junior does not possess, and consequently, like a strong dose of medicine which must be taken without water, his letters have to be swallowed "neat" and like that same medicine after being "taken" they give you something to think about, though I'm bound to say that they have no nasty taste behind them. However I may hear from him next mail and until then "Dum Spiro Spero," as Louis says.

Our Regiment or "Contingent" as you always call it in New Zealand is sadly thinned out now as far as fighting strength goes and I don't think half of the fellows are with us at the present time. Some dead, some wounded, many in hospital and a whole lot waiting in Newcastle for remounts. We may possibly have some or all of the last mentioned with us before many days but I can't say that with any certainty as I don't know.

As Lottie says our 7th has been in a good many hot shops but we have served half our time now so our luck may change. Chaps who joined us from other Contingents say that since they have been with us they have seen more actual fighting than they ever saw with their own.

Soldier Boy

Of course if you people in NZ were to say that to some returned Troopers they would call me a perverter of the truth but it's a fact and those of the men I mentioned who live to get back will say it themselves when the time comes.

We've had six months of it now and it's been scrapping nearly all the time and will be for the next six and even then we will leave plenty of fighting behind us.

So often I wish that I had brought a small camera out here with me. I could have worked it fine and if I wouldn't have had a few things and places to show you tell me. I would like particularly to let you have a look at our nigger orderlies and cooks etc. Every squadron is allowed to keep two nigger boys on Government rations, for their own use. These boys are usually picked up from Kaffif Kraals on the march and come to us without a name and unable to speak a word of English. The first item is to name them and this is usually done by reeling off about a dozen different names and making the newcomer understand what is required and select one. In this way we have darkies priding themselves with all sorts of appellations, Scriptural and otherwise. With us we have niggers called "Solomon, Peter, Pat, Yankee, Jim, Snowball, Pikanin, De Wet, Matthew, Luke, Snowdrop, Blackfeet," etc every one of whom thinks his and his only the best name of them all.

The dress of these swarthy little gentlemen the camera might portray but the pen never, for some are half dressed, some three quarters, a few, whole, and a good many not at all, and yet taken all round they are as happy and light-hearted a lot as you could possibly find. As such we will leave them and I must leave this for today so Adieu, "Aah Koana" as the niggers say.

Tuesday Morning 19ᵗʰ November

I am going to add a little more now though it is only by the barest chance that I am in a position to do any writing today for at one o'clock this morning we were turned out to go on a night march and try and surround some Boers by day-break.

Of course, I was bundled out with the rest but after I hustled about after horse feed, rations and such like the Sergt came to me and another chap who had just got over the dysentery and told us that as there was more fit men than horses we could go back to bed again and somebody else could ride our horses.

This morning when I woke up I found the sun shining high in the heavens, or it seemed high, for I had done a lay in until half past five. I turned out, did the usual stretch and commenced to look around for signs of breakfast. After a considerable expenditure of time and words I secured a mug of cocoa and a bit of fried meat and biscuit so I have had quite a high feed this morning.

Needless to say I would not have got this under usual circumstances, but as all, or nearly all, the Mounted troops are out and our Non Coms are with them I am for the time being my own boss and could battle for my stomach myself and when I do that ten-to-one I don't go so very hungry. This is just such a morning as makes a chap glad to be alive. A beautiful blue sky with just a few hazy morning clouds over the horizon, and shading off the more distant ranges and kopjes into a dreamy and misty blue, while everything near can be seen with the distinctness of a Canterbury Nor-West morning.

When we were camped here last time we had one very exciting night. Scouts coming in brought word that Boers were concentrating on the camp and would probably attack in the small hours of the morning. Fatigue parties were sent out in the darkness to dig trenches and nearly every man jack of us who was armed, officers and all slept in full rig with bayonets fixed and rifles by our sides, in a huge ring which stretched completely round the camp about two chains inside the usual outposts.

Of course we eagerly awaited the arrival of our guests and we had everything so thoroughly ready for them that we were hoping that they would put in an appearance.

I had been on outpost all the night before so I lay down behind an anthill and was sound asleep in no time but – those who kept awake had quite a flutter of excitement about two in the morning when they heard a bullet whistle and a rifle crack. They passed the word around that Jackie was coming but it was only a sentry firing at a mule or something.

Meanwhile I slept for I was tired and didn't care if all the Boers between there and Koomati Poort were on to us. Next morning we were mounted and off on day post at four and it was then that we ran into Mr Jackie on Gelak Hill and our two fellows were killed. They (the Boers) had got round us alright but had not attacked which was very fortunate for themselves on this occasion.

Just a few yards away from me is one of our fellows trying to impress upon the fertile mind of our nigger Pat the enormous size of the steamer in which we came here. Poor Pat can't take it in. "How big" he says. "Was it big as four wagons."

"Bigger" says our chap. "It hold 700 men and long as here to there;" pointing to an anthill about eighty yards away. Poor Pat rolls his eyes in disbelief and turns away saying "You white fellow tell plenty much big'd lie" and thus closes the controversy. These niggers have some very quaint sayings and bring them out in a way that would make the soberest laugh.

It's very amusing too to hear these dusky brethren of ours when they quarrel amongst themselves which they often do. The abuse they use and the way they use it, to say nothing about the looks of scorn and hatred which go along with it would make a cat laugh. One will call the other a "Big ugly black faced niggah" which other will retort by calling his offender "A dirty feeted, bared-legged Kaffir and black man's dog" etc etc. It's pot and kettle in real life when they start, but they soon make it up again and in a few minutes, time are dancing together or eating out of the same bowl.

Some of them are very religious in their way and their views and ideas on that subject, if it were not for their sincerity would be most comical. One fellow told me that "God live in dah sky, Him plenty much big Baas. Him Colonel. Got plenty wagon plenty wings and plenty much bullock and mules." "Jesus him Captain, Got plenty angels and he fly about with dem to look for black man. Bye-um-bye he catch me and take me to Heaven." "Dah Debil he lib in Hell. He Got plenty much fire plenty smoke, plenty horns plenty forks and plenty assagai. He fly about and catch dah Dutchman. He no good."

This same chap would go and swear at the bullocks like a trooper and when he came back he would fold his hands and with the most pious face imaginable would say "When I die I go to Heben; Ise welly good man."

November 21ˢᵗ

And here's for another little flutter with the pencil, though I must not let this letter run me into many more leaves or else I will undoubtedly run a serious risk of wearying your patience and my own too.

Now Mother if what I write today is a bit mixed as regards grammar and a bit hard to decipher I must beg to be forgiven on the usual grounds of "tiredness" for yesterday morning my Squadron was turned out at a quarter to three and from four AM until sunset we were on "day post" around the camp watching for Mr Jackie. We got back into camp about dark and after drawing rations etc I expect I got to bed somewhere around 9 o'clock. Then fifty men were picked out for another "surprise party", and I was amongst the number.

At half past eleven we were bundled out of bed, saddled up in a cutting cold wind and punctually at midnight we moved out into the night. I have described a night march before so I need not go into details concerning this one.

We came on the Boers about an hour before daybreak but found them prepared for us. Rifles flashed, bullets flew, one man hit. We took cover and waited for daylight. In the meantime the Boers did a mike and when morning dawned after patrolling the hills there was nothing for us to do but return to camp. This we did, arriving here some time after eight o'clock I think it was. Usual camp work follows but in spite of all I have had half an hour's much needed sleep and a bite of dinner so now here I am blinking and nodding like a frightened more pork, but I know you will look over such blunders as I am sure to make.

I'll lay this aside again now Mother and with your consent snatch another forty winks beside my mates here who are forgetting all cares in the blissful unconsciousness of Blanket Bay.

Au Revoir

Tuesday Evening

My Dear Mother
All unexpectedly we have just got another mail and my word I'm in luck again. I got a Canterbury, a letter from Lottie, one from yourself and one from Jessie. Thanks for paper with pictures of the CMR [Canterbury Mounted Rifles] they are a fine body of men aren't they I'm one; see. Can't answer your letter in full now but glad and thankful that you are able to get up at 3.30 and do surprise cleaning. Glad Jessie is so well and happy.

Heaps of Love from
Harry

Soldier Boy

Dear Old Sis

Just a word for your dear old self. Many thanks for your kind and welcome letter which I can't answer in full. Orders have just come to be ready to march at 4.30 in the morning so I have no chance to write much and I want to send another letter to Jessie too I'm not going War Correspondents cause they get cussed more than enough out here. Many thanks for letters and good wishes and don't go getten into a ghost or I'll disown you when I come back. Oh Glorious dream. 28 breakfasts in bed. That's worth living for. Reveille early and moving once again. Here we have no continuing city no country either. Heaps of love to you from

HGG

November 21ˢᵗ (About 10 minutes later)

I just got word that Col Porter is expected tomorrow, and that a detachment of seventy men is to go into Vryheid to meet him tomorrow morning and take in half a dozen wagons. I have been doing the right thing after all in bustling with my letter. I thought something of this sort would happen and I was quite right as I'll get this away now. I'm sorry I can't send a line to Lottie and all the rest but it's no good I can't. You will have to make this go all round. I'm afraid that some of my correspondence will have to be neglected for I have a good many writing to me now and I can't stand sending "notes" to anyone. I like to send a letter or nothing. I think several will have to be content with nothing. Give my love to Good Old Mrs Cromie and tell her that I don't forget her, and appreciate her kind thoughts and memories about myself. I must stop now.

Best Love from
Harry

Patriotism was a strong force in the nineteenth century and posters such as this would have been a common sight when Harry Gilbert signed up to fight. (Courtesy Hocken Library, Dunedin)

Pandawana
November 25th 1901

Dear Mother

When answering yours yesterday I completely forgot to mention one thing which you were speaking about and that is about our coming home. You say that you have seen notice that the Contingent is to be home in January.

Now Mother don't let yourself be tricked into believing those sorts of things no matter how many papers they appear in. I don't want to disappoint you but it will be best for you to know straight away that I have it on good authority that we haven't the faintest hope of being in New Zealand before next June or May at the latest or earliest I should say. These stories about going home are always flying about and we have heard about it and had the date fixed about our times since we came out here but they are absolutely without foundation of any sort.

We have signed on for twelve months service and we started on May 11th when we landed here or at least that's the way I take it if it should be otherwise our year will date from April 1st and then we will get back in May. That is of course those of us who are spared. That goes without saying doesn't it. We hear yarns about mobilising continually. In fact they get into the wind very regularly and one is going about now that we will get home in March but its all bunkum for there's too many stray Boers wandering about this country for them to send us away with our length of service incompleted.

I know this sort of news will seem cruel to you but I think it is best that you should know instead of building up false hopes which must be dashed to the ground at last. I can ease your mind in one direction though and that is I can tell you that all this time will not be spent on the veldt and we have considerably over half our time in now and by the time you get this (January I expect) we won't have so very much more trecking to do.

You will think by what I have told you that I am not sorry about not going home sooner. As I said in my letter yesterday I would be very glad to be back but if I'm spared I'm going to put in my time our here. I don't want you people to continue thinking that I am sorry that I ever saw SA for I'm not a bit. If anyone asked me about coming out here I'd certainly tell them to stay at home but for myself I'm quite content to see my term through and whether I sign on after this is over remains to be seen.

I got a ducking last night and have a lot more to get yet and if in the face of these I can say that I don't whip the cat it's not fair for you at home to think that I do and if I did who would I have to thank for it all. Surely no-one but myself and I'm not going to put my fingers into the fire, with my eyes open and then grumble because I find it hot. I didn't come out here expecting to sleep on a sofa and be fed on jam tarts although I didn't quite expect to be starved or nearly so but speaking of that I can say that we are doing better for rations just at present.. Don't worry about me for I'm alright and just be content to let fate work out her own plans and it'll all come right at last.

I think that is all so once again I'll say Goodbye and ask you to write soon to

Your Aff Son
HG Gilbert

Column's Camp, about 6 miles from Vryheid
December 1ˢᵗ 1901

Dear Mother

We got to this place tonight and as the whole column is not going into town tomorrow but only a part of it with the convoy and that at 3AM I am taking this, a last chance to drop another line to you. Our mail closes at ten o'clock tonight and for the sake of those who desire to do any writing we have leave to keep our lights going until then but as a general thing and for precaution's sake all camp lights have to be out by half past six now.

I intended to write a letter to Dad and Lottie this mail but as usual it has been impossible for me to do it as it's only by making use of spare moments that I have this lot finished. However you can tell them both that theirs is the next letter, I will make a start at if I'm spared.

Oddly, after writing so many letters in pencil, Harry reverted here to the use of a dip-pen and indian ink, even though it was apparently written in haste.

Soldier Boy

I know Lottie in particular will think me awful mean but I can't help it for to tell the truth my correspondence is getting the whip hand of me, and as we are moving night and day now letter writing is a business I can tell you.

It's thundering and lightning now at top and raining too but I'm alright for that now as another chap and myself have sewn two of our blankets together and made a "Bivie" as such things are called out here.

By the time you get this Christmas will have come and gone. I hope you will have a good time. Tell me all about it when you write.

We have had a good bit of fighting this last week and today in particular. Six of the Queenslanders were caught and stripped of their gear and clothes and came in tonight in Boer rig.

All of us doing service out here are to get a pound of pudding, a pint of beer and a quarter of a pound of tobacco served out to us for a Christmas box so we are not going to fare so badly after all, but it will make the biscuits taste nasty on Boxing day I'm afraid but we don't worry about that.

I'll have to stop now or I'll go to sleep over this and the light is flickering too.

Here are the reveilles for the week ending today so you can judge for yourself:
Monday 12:30AM, Tuesday 2AM, Wed. 3AM, Thursday 12 (Midnight) Friday 2:30AM, Saturday 4AM and this morning 3:30 so if I and the rest haven't got reason to feel sleepy nobody has.

I must stop now. Write soon, and tell the ones who don't get a letter this time not to blame me too much for rifles and pens won't work together. Forgive this scribbling this time and hope for better next from

Your Aff Son
Harry

In the small blank space at the top of the letter, Harry added this succinct note.

We have been on two third rations for this last two days and have to remain on them until wagons get back from Vryheid. At present 10 shillings for a rice pudding and a cup of sweet tea.

Adieu

About 6 miles from Dryheid
December 1st 1901

Dear Mother,

We got to this place tonight & as the whole column is not going into the town tomorrow but only a part of it with the convoy & that at three A.M. I am taking this, a last chance to drop another line [to] you. Our mail closes at ten o'clock tonight & for the sake of those who desire to do any writing we have leave to keep our lights going until then. but as a general thing & for precaution's sake all camp lights have to be out by half past — now. I intended to write a letter to Dad & Lottie this mail but as usual it has been impossible for me to do it as it's only by making use of spare moments that I have this lot finished. However you can tell them both that theirs is the next letters I will make a start at it I'm afraid. I know Lottie in particular will think me awful mean but I can't help it for to tell the truth my correspondence is getting the whip hand of me & as we are moving night & day now letter writing is a business I can tell you. It's thundering & lightening now & [?] & raining too but I'm alright for that now as another chap & myself have sewn two our blankets together & made a 'Bivie' as

On The Veldt
December 3rd 1901

Dear Lottie

I'm going to write like the very mischief and try to get a few lines done to put in along with Dad before my light is spotted. I'm afraid that this will only be a disappointment to you after promising a decent letter next time but you know Lot necessity knows no law. I was up at two this morning on the treck at four and have to be going again at three tomorrow to say nothing about all the early and late shifts we have been doing lately. It is very tiring.

I don't know whether we are moving tomorrow but I think we must be or else we would not be about so soon. I had a great indirect compliment paid to me last mail for both Spencer's and Condon's people were reckoning them up for not writing oftener and they wound up almost in the same words with "Harry Gilbert's people get a lot of letters from him" so I plume myself a bit now though it's a compliment well paid for I fear.

We have been having some lively goes with the Boers about here lately and last Sunday had a lively time in the rear. Two Queenslanders were hit and half a dozen

On The Veldt —

Dec 3rd
1901

Dear Lottie,

I'm going to write like the very mischief & try & get a few lines done to put in along with Dad's before my light is spotted. I'm afraid that this will only be a dissapointment to you after promising a decent letter next time but you know that necessity knows no law. I was up at two this morning on the trek at four & have to be going again at three tomorrow to say nothing about all the early & late shifts we have been going lately. It is very tiring. I dont know whether we are moving tomorrow but I think we must be or else we would not be about so soon. I had a great indirect complement paid to me last mail for both Spencer's & Gordon's people were reckoning them up for not writing oftener & they wound up almost in the same words with "Harry Gilbert's people get a lot of letters from him." So I plume myself a bit now though its a complement well paid for I fear. We have been having some lively goes with the Boers about here lately & last Sunday had a lively time in the taken prisoners. Six Boers were killed and eight or nine wounded but this will make you creepy rather than be of interest so I will drop it. Our Seventh is having a busy time of it all round one way and another. We have lost about 15 killed and over forty wounded and yet people told us that we were coming over here to act the gentleman as all the fighting was over. Some of us however thought different and we were right. They will not be able to call those of us who get back Tin Soldiers that's one thing certain and we will be able to rub it in to those who win battles innumerable over a pint of beer and capture De Wet while lying on their backs and feeling in the air for the earth. Now Lot you must pardon me I'm honour bright too tired to do anything but sleep and my lines and letters are wandering all over the paper like a school kid's. It makes me wild to send little notes like this but what's a fellow to do, it's only common courtesy to answer letters received but I'm afraid I'll have to give it up before long as soldiering and writing will not go together. Take heaps of love from your blinking and nodding Bro.

Harry

Orange River Colony Standing Camp, Green's Drift

December 16th 1901
For All Hands again

Dear All

Harry took a week to write this abridged letter that describes the lead-up to Christmas on the veld.

As another opportunity for writing has presented itself I am going to make another start with a letter and get as much done as time will admit of. You will see by the heading that we are in the State again. At present we are clearing the country and acting as guard and fighting column to a party of engineers who are constructing a line of Blockhouses from Ingogo. I believe we are going to take them right through to a place called Vrede about thirty or fourty miles from here.

Orange River Colony

Landing Camp.   Green's Drift.
                                                    (Very nice place)

On All Hands again   16/12/01 —
                    Dear All.
                              As another opportunity for
writing has presented itself I am going to make
another start with a letter & get as much done as time
will admit of. You will see by the heading that we
are in the State again. At present we are clearing
the country & acting as guard & fighting column to a
party of engineers who are constructing a line of
Blockhouses from Ingogo. I believe we are going
to take them right through to a place called Vrede
about thirty or fourty miles from here. If that is so
it means Christmas on the Veldt for us. In fact I
think that is already a certainty as our waggons
left here this morning to go to Newcastle for
more rations & our Christmas grants if they are
available so I think all hope of being in a town
that occasion is dead. I guess it wont make
much difference anyhow — as no matter where we are
we will be surrounded with what the Rev. Stubbs is
pleased to call the "Rattle & Bustle of arms" & we may
as well have that on the Veldt as anywhere. Since
writing my last I have nothing peck in particular to
tell you. We have been doing as is our wont —
making night marches & getting slap when we are
there. We made one on Saturday night. Being rooted out

Soldier Boy

If that is so it means Christmas on the veldt for us. In fact I think that is already a certainty as our wagons left here this morning to go to Newcastle for more rations and our Christmas grants if they are available. So I think all hope of being in a town on that occasion is dead.

I guess it won't make much difference anyhow as no matter where we are we will be surrounded with what the Rev Stubbs is pleased to call the "Rattle and Bustle of arms" and we may as well have that on the veldt as anywhere.

Another of our Cant. Boys has been sent into the line dangerously ill with the Enteric Fever. He has had a bad dose and i'ts ten chances to one if it doesn't pass him out as he is a big fat fellow, and just the sort that it plays up with. His name is Revell; you will see by the papers how things are with him before this reaches you.

There was great excitement in our lines on Saturday evening when a small mail arrived and one of our chaps was the happy receiver of a parcel of Christmas gifts including a nice tidy little plum pudding. Needless to say he was soon surrounded by a crowd of admiring and hungry eyed "pals" and was the hero of the hour but his prized possession was not long in returning into its case as while visible its existence was not much of a certainty and it was in the gravest danger of being devoured at any moment. That one lucky beggar will have home made duff for dinner anyhow and that is a thing which will be mightily scarce with us all this year however "Dum Spiro Spero" and fight on.

We are being greatly troubled with mosquitos out here and my face is just knotted all over with their bites. Little pests of this sort when their efforts are seconded by the attacks of other insects which live in the wrinkles and seams of our clothes, and with which we have all been swarming for the last month or two make life very lively now. Sleeping all in one piece is bad enough in the cold weather but now, well, it hain't nice, but troubles were made for soldiers, soldiers were made for fighting, and fighting was made for fools they say, so we must not grumble at our fare for there's a good time coming.

I'm going to stop for dinner now and in case you might like to know what that consists of I can tell you that I have a pint and a half of tea (so called) and to eat I have a biscuit, not an Aulsebrook sweet and sugar topped but a hard, square, tasteless, brown, saw dustified military bullet stopper, the sort you can pave back yards with or render horses senseless by hitting them between the eyes with the same. Amen.

With the_____

Compliments of the Season . . .

From the

**Burgesses and Residents of
Durban and Newcastle . . .**

Field Force. Xmas 1901

South Africa

One of these accompanied each parcel which
contained 1 Towel 1 Packet Stationery. Pound Tobacco,
2 Pipes 12 Packets Cigarettes, 1 Book 1 Cake Chocolate —
1 Pound Plum Pudding & a Pack of Cards. Needless to
say all of the above was thankfully received by.
Those at The Front —

To :- Members of all the Columns.
Operating in Natal in Dec 1901.

Among the labels that Harry sent home from South Africa was one from the "Burgesses and
Residents of Durban and Newcastle".

Soldier Boy

Friday December 20th

I am going to do a bit more to this. We are still at the blockhouse work and to all appearances are likely to be so for some time to come and taken all round it is the easiest time we have had since we started on the treck. We merely keep pace with the Engineers moving about every third day and then only going about 5 miles.

There are a few Boers knocking about here now and sniping is much indulged in with our day posts. On Tuesday four of us were sent out mounted to guard a wagon of dismounted fatigue men who were going to a farm house for some wood. Some Boers tried to cut us off and only by vigorous galloping, we succeeded in beating them, getting to a rocky position which they were making for just before them for once. However, had we been five minutes later things would have been very different for us and our wagon.

The next day we were Day outpost and the post I was on consisted of four men and we were sent, thanks to the thickheadedness of one of our officers, away to kingdom come on a ridge fully 3 miles away. We hadn't been there half an hour before we began to see the Boers gathering in two's and threes, here there and everywhere and trying to cut us off from the camp. This was the simplest thing in the world to do as we were in a rotten position and couldn't get half a view. We stayed as long as we dared and then we had to retire back towards the camp or else we must all have been captured or shot as the only place were where the Boers were in view from our camp was too close to our position to allow the artillery to get fairly on to them without danger to us.

As soon as we retired the Colonel sent a galloper out to see how things were and soon after the guns [were] working on the ridges around. We had one man wounded that day, pretty badly and one horse shot dead but we captured a big mob of Boer horses.

This morning our Convoy arrived bringing in our Christmas Grants of Beer and Pudding and our Christmas mail. Great joy was caused among a good many who were fortunate enough to get cards and presents from those at home. Here you'd see one chap sneaking into a quiet corner with a card from some fair maiden over the water, while another would be dead to the world in the blissful perusal of a scented and delicately shaded note in a girl's hand-writing and elaborately sprinkled with xxxxxx's in every spare corner. Another chap rejoiced over the arrival of a beautiful little "hold all" just no size but full of such things as needles, thread, buttons, pins, and other small but extremely useful articles not forgetting some soft white cloth for field dressing. This needless to say was from his Mother and will be more useful to him and a good many more than all the cards and scented letters on the column, though these are very welcome over in a place and in such surroundings as this. Maybe I think this the more as I didn't get any myself having instead to witness the pleasure of others.

I thought that I might possibly get a Christmas greeting from some of you but I can't say that I expected it as it is a long way to send such things from NZ to South Africa. It's just as well that I didn't for I didn't get even a line from a single soul let alone a packet or parcel. However you must not think that I am disappointed. I know all the same that I am not forgotten or I think that I'm not at anyrate and even if I have slipped your memory slightly I have only myself to thank and I'll get some more letters from you later on so I must for the time being forget NZ and all that in it is, forget that I was ever anything else but a dirty trooper and during that space of forgetfulness I must do my duty and get gloriously drunk in approved Tommy style so that when the holiday season is past and we are once more on short rations I will be able to look back and know that my soldier's Xmas on the veldt was spent in soldier fashion and that the most was made of my share of good things while they lasted.

The night we left Newcastle we were fairly out on our ace for sleeping accommodation. All the troops and wagons moved off at 4 in the morning with the exception of Canterbury Coy which stayed to escort the ox convoy. This was still loading when the column moved, but it was supposed to be on the road at ten. However it didn't start until one in the afternoon and consequently we could not overtake the main body that night so at Fort Botha we laagered up and camped. Our blankets, dixies and rations were on the squadron wagon which went with the column and so we were in it.

With their characteristic good nature the Tommies at the fort gave us some of their wood supply and the lend of their dixies to make tea in and so by raiding some of the convoy we were escorting we did alright for tea and then we put on our great coats and with our heads buried under our saddles, ostrich fashion, we laid down on the earth for the night. Some sang, some slept and some didn't. I did and well but I woke up suffering from that want of heat which had kept many of my mates awake and which with no blankets under or above you and with a clear cold wind whistling round the saddle flaps, is mighty hard to get rid of. However morning came and with it heat, so that trouble was soon over and then the colonial spirit gave vent to itself in a burst of song, for once a trouble ceases it is as good as forgotten out here.

Now I must stop for today and perhaps I won't write any more until after Christmas only a day or two off now. It seems hardly possible but so it is.

Until next time
Adieu

Sunday 22ⁿᵈ December

I have just had breakfast (2PM) and I am going to do a little bit more to this. You will be a little surprised to see me having my morning meal at such a late hour and no doubt on first thought you will conclude that I have been having a rare old lay in. However, such is far from being the case as I have been away with the mounted troops and artillery since three oclock this morning.

As a rule we don't have to start this sort of work on an absolutely empty stomach but this morning the Horse Picket did a lay in and we were roused just ten minutes before moving off time. What sort of a flutter we got on then I won't try to describe but saddles flew on to the horses you may guess. By three we were away and even then we had to do a gallop in the dark to overtake the guns.

Well we cruised about and captured some cattle and sheep, shot a lot of horses and then "came home to breakfast" at the hour stated and all very fit for it we were which goes without saying. The reason we were out so eagerly this morning is a sad one for yesterday afternoon about 30 Boers sprang a march on, and captured three of our scouts and a Queenslander and one of our niggers who were outside our day posts at some Kaffir kraals. That was not so bad, but the cold-blooded curs stood the poor nigger up and shot him like a dog in cold blood. They also mortally wounded another nigger who tried to escape.

I know this will be sickening news to you all, but I tell you this so you can see what sort of demons we are fighting. The field cornet who was in charge of the Boers told our chaps that if he ever caught any of us out with black scouts he would shoot them all white and black too, but once let them come that game and their cake will be dough in quick sticks for every one we get of them will share the same fate and they can't afford that. But they won't try it they know too well what it would mean for themselves.

The ambulance went out last night for the dead and wounded Kaffirs and I saw them when they came back and if ever I felt bitter against the Boer race I did when I gazed down on the stiff and stark nigger who they had so cruelly and uselessly done to death. The wounded one they found walking into camp despite the fact that he had a bullet right through his head and another through his shoulder. He was awfully game but he died at 5 o'clock this morning and both he and his mate were buried in one grave this morning while we were out looking for their murderers, for they were nothing else.

If ever you hear any of our Pro Boer friends sticking up for the Boers just read this out to them and tell them from me that they want to be out here and suffer the same fate and if I had my way they would be too. The Boers have absolutely no excuse for this kind of conduct, as the niggers, as a whole, are practically a neutral people, and in any numbers do not assist either side, while black scouts are employed by both parties and yet whenever they catch ours they shoot them like dogs the despicable curs.

It's done simply for spite nothing else for the average Boer thinks no more of a darkie than he does of a dog, often times not so much. However, if ever the black livered gentlemen who did this deed dropped into our hands and are recognised they will have mighty quick passage over the Jordan and God have mercy on them for our chaps will have none and little wonder.

As for the Pro Boer fraternity I'd have every man jack of them black and sent out as scouts and let the Jackies capture them and then while they were backed up against a stone wall with a rifle levelled at their heads I'd quietly ask them if Mr Boer was the merciful and God-fearing man they always cracked him up to be and then probably they'd see things in a different light. But I suppose I have said enough on this subject, perhaps more than I ought to have said but it will serve at anyrate to dispel any lingering doubts which you may have had in your minds as to the right and justice of the cause for which we are fighting.

What I have told you must not make you any the more concerned as to my own personal safety as this sort of thing has been going on for over a twelve month now though this is the first case that has come directly under my notice and I hope never to see another, and at any rate I am just as safe here as I would be in Canterbury for that matter, for I am convinced that even in war men are not killed at haphazard, but that each one has his length of time to live and if he has to be shot at the end of that time he'll be shot even if he gets down a well to escape the lead and if he isnt to be shot all the bullets made will fly wide of him though of course, when the bullets are flying the uncertainty of the things causes some amount of fidgeting. Howsom ever I've said enough about this sort of thing so I'll turn to something more interesting.

It's just two days to Christmas and this being Sunday while we were asleep last night thousands in NZ in their various churches were singing "Hark the Herald Angels Sing", and listening to the discourses re the Advent of One whose mission was to bring "Peace on Earth." When will that peace come about and put an end to all the miseries and cruelties of war.

Really war is an unreasonable business when you come to think of it. Perhaps today a man comes in under a white flag; we ride out and meet him. He may not be a bad sort of a fellow, and we talk about the weather and such like things in a most friendly way. He rides away and tomorrow we are shooting at the same chap and he at us each trying to put out the other's lights. There's no sense in it when you look at it in this light and yet nothing short of war will settle some disputes so while we have a hand in it we must do our best and as Cromwell said "Trust in God and keep our powder dry."

There'll be an end to all things some day and no doubt there'll be an end to this affair though it's a mighty long time coming about. I'll stop now until after Christmas when I will conclude this rambling offusion.

Dryhoek, Xmas Night

Christmas has come and is just about gone and here I am going to put a final touch to my letter. I have to be up and out on day post at four tomorrow morning so have not got time to finish in much style and will leave a description of my Xmas for some future date. I didn't get drunk and had a fair feed so can't complain. I wonder how things are in Cust. Good I hope. Have just heard that an 8th is leaving NZ.

Goodbye. Best love
Harry

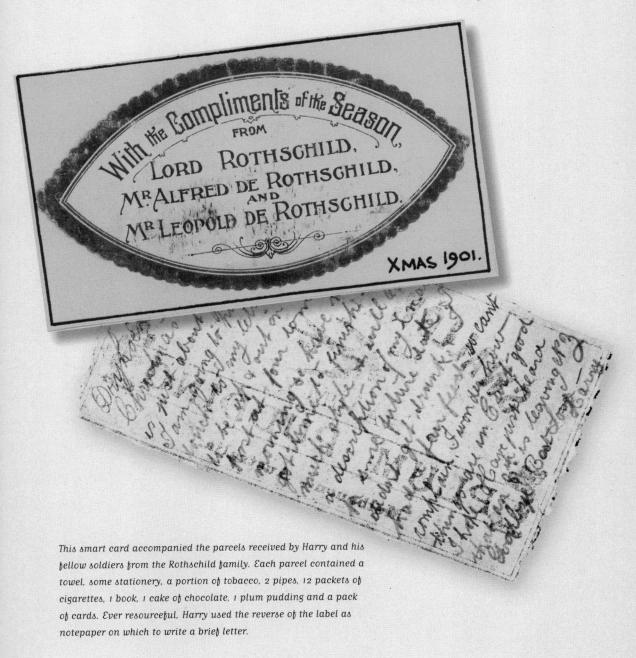

With the Compliments of the Season,
FROM
LORD ROTHSCHILD,
MR ALFRED DE ROTHSCHILD,
AND
MR LEOPOLD DE ROTHSCHILD.

XMAS 1901.

This smart card accompanied the parcels received by Harry and his
fellow soldiers from the Rothschild family. Each parcel contained a
towel, some stationery, a portion of tobacco, 2 pipes, 12 packets of
cigarettes, 1 book, 1 cake of chocolate, 1 plum pudding and a pack
of cards. Ever resourceful, Harry used the reverse of the label as
notepaper on which to write a brief letter.

Orange River Colony.

Schuyfort —

Jan 3rd 190-

My Dear Father & Mother.

    I have had no mail from anyone for near
a month but still I am going to make a start at another
letter to you & send it away when I can. We are still at
this Blockhouse work & are not very far from Drede now
if our guide is to be relied on but for all we know we may
have to take them on past there. I sent a letter away to
you on Christmas night or rather Boxing Day morning &
hope you will get it before this arrives I think I told
in it that the Boers have been very busy with us since
we got past Bothas Fort — I told you about them capturing
some of our Scouts & shooting the niggers didn't I & I believe
I promised to tell you about how I spent my Christmas
Well that can be quickly told as it was very much like
most other days are out here excepting that we fared
better for "Chuck" Getting up time was as usual at four
& all the usual work had to be done but on this certain
day it was intermingled with hearty handshakes &
congratulations from "Pals" & "Merry Christmas" were flying
about all roads I may just mention here that a week or
two ago I had a letter from Nelson of the R W Kents —
he along with other things said "I wish you a Merry Xmas
old chap though I know very well that you wont find
it if you are on the Veldt" Such I may say was the
real meaning of all the "Wishes" this year & it was more
a matter of form than reality for we all know what to
expect

Orange River Colony, Tehujfort
January 3rd 1902

My Dear Father and Mother

I have had no mail from anyone for nearly a month but still I am going to make a start at another letter to you and send it away when I can. We are still at this blockhouse work and are not very far from Vride if our guide is to be relied on but for all we know we may have to take them on past there.

I sent a letter away to you on Christmas night or rather Boxing Day morning and I hope you will get it before this arrives. I think I told you in it that the Boers have been very busy with us since we got past Botha Fort. I told you about them capturing some of our Scouts and shooting the niggers didn't I and I believe I promised to tell you how I spent my Christmas. Well that can be quickly told for it was very much like most other days out here excepting that we fared better for "Chuck".

Getting up time was as usual at four and all the usual work had to be done but on this certain day it was intermingled with hearty handshakes and congratulations from "Pals" and "Merry Christmases" were flying about all roads.

However putting two and two together we fared better than I had anticipated when I heard for a certainty that we were to pass it on the veldt. Dinner was on this, as on all Christmas Days, the most important and agreeable item and I must devote a few minutes to a description of this part of the programme and its preparation.

As our good luck had it we were camped not very far from some Kaffir Kraals and another place not very far away was the home of a potato patch so by putting these two facts together you will be in a position to conclude that we were not going to starve. From the Kaffirs we were able, at trifling expense (to those who had money which I had not) to procure a few lean pigs and some fowls. I did not bother the razor-backed and bird-caged ribbed former, but after a big blarney and by dint of much persuasive and forcible logic my mate managed to secure something like a twelve-year-old hen and thus "Chicken Soup" for dinner was a certainty. The making of this was left to my culinary skill and how worthily I performed the task I leave to yourselves to judge.

My first trouble was to secure a pot. The word secure in this case means to steal as that was the only thing possible at such a time. After marching up and down a

Soldier Boy

time or two and keeping my eyes about me I was able to swoop down on a big open stew pan without a lid and my "chicken" was on the fire in quick sticks. As a cook out here never knows how soon he may have to leave his work it behoves him to make the most of spare moments. This I did by filling the pot up at once with spuds and the compressed vegetables which are occasionally supplied to us and which contained chopped up and dried, cabbage, carrots, turnips, potatoes, and other mysterious and concentrated concerns which for want of knowledge I cannot name but they must be plants of some kind as the label on the tins declares that nothing but "vegetables" are included in this "choice mixture".

Well having got this far with my soup I was able to sit by and contemplate that it had four hours to boil and that by that time it would be real good. Then up came a wind and the ashes began to fly and I was forced to keep a spoon in hand to scoop off such of them as would blow into my lidless pan. About an hour of this and up comes an indignant individual with "Hey, Gilbert what the H--- are you at with my pot." "What pot?" says I. "Just as if you don't know whose it is. Come to light now and get that old fowl out of it. I want to use it myself." "You go to blazes," says I. "This is my Christmas dinner and I'm not going to empty it out now." "I'll see about that," says he. "You knew D--- well it was mine so you empty it quick and dirty." "I'll do nothing of the kind," says I, "and I did not know it was yours." "Yes you did." "No I didn't." "Oh but you did." "I tell you I did not. Do you think that when I go out to steal a pot I hold it up and ask whose it is. You must think Im an ass."

This bit of logic on my part made the aggrieved one laugh and so it was arranged that by giving him a leg of "Chicken" at dinner time I could keep the pot and off he goes with "You were a bit swift for me Gilbert D--- you but I'll dish some one else for theirs before long. Merry Christmas." Thus one crime led to another but what was that to me when I had a Christmas Dinner at stake.

About ten oclock all hands had to parade for Divine Service on the veldt and so cooking had to be left for awhile. As we sang Christmas hymns and listened to a few remarks on "Peace of Earth, Goodwill to men" I in common with many another could not help thinking of many other Christmases which I had spent in very different surroundings to these.

But the Chaplain had a word to suit the occasion "As you stand here" he said "Don't think that because you are miles away out on the veldt, all by yourselves as it were that you are forgotten. It is not so. Before you were awakened this morning prayers had gone up for you all from thousands of homes in Queensland and New Zealand and before the sun sets this evening, in thousands of Churches the world over you will be remembered at the throne of Grace where prayers are presented and mercies asked for 'Those at the Front'."

He got no further for the Boers attacked our outposts. We were ordered to "Stand to Arms". The inlying squadron galloped out so Church broke up. The Boers were soon put to flight and I got back in time to skim a layer of ashes from the top of my soup. In due time dinner time came and in spite of everything dinner was a merry meal. My chicken soup was a veritable bog of potatoes and cabbage and soup there was none. The "Chicken" was the toughest I ever ate, but the plum pudding was good and so was the ration of Beer so we were all filled and had to spare. One or two made fools of themselves by getting drunk but they were very few, and I don't think that there was more than three fights all day. That night singing was very much indulged in and Christmas hymns were sang over and over again until silence finally settled down on the camp.

On Boxing day the Column moved and we were up at two o'clock so we were soon back in the old groove again. Since then we have had a busy and sad time.

The night after Christmas we marched out at ten o'clock to look for bother. Only mounted troops went of course. I don't know how far we travelled but just before daybreak a thick fog settled down and we halted and as usual half of us lay down and fell asleep. Of what happened to others I don't know so much but I will tell you my own experiences. I fell asleep with the rest but for once I woke up without being called. I stood up leaning on my rifle and remarked to some mates that day was breaking and that the fog was still very thick. My horse had wandered and I had just looked round for it where there came a crack and a crash of rifles, a hiss and howl of bullets.

I don't think I can hope to describe what followed. Fellows jumped up half asleep, horses which were struck reared and fell or else made off full gallop. Then came another volley and the mad stampede started. Men and horses racing for their lives. For me to lay down was madness for I saw a troop of riderless horses of the 14 Hussars coming straight for me through the fog so I made off at top. It was a terrible five minutes. As I ran one poor chap of the Hussars, with a short sharp groan threw up his hands and fell like a post, dead, shot through the head. Horses with the blood streaming from them, neighed, staggered and dropped among us. A bit further on I was side by side with another chap, both going full speed when with another moan another poor chap, a New Zealander of our own Squadron staggered and fell right in our path. To stop was impossible so I dodged and the other chap sprang over the prostrate and groaning man and kept on our course.

When we got to cover with the first fright over we were quickly got into fighting trim. Ranks were formed and with a cheer and a roar ridges were rushed and taken, the Boers making off. The packhorse with the two cases of ammunition was laying dead but the cartridges were quickly dumped into a square and all were got ready to make a stand. After about half an hour's straggling firing the Boers were ousted with two killed and three prisoners in our hands, their wounded unknown.

The fog cleared off and the sun shone out and what a sight met our eyes. It was like a miniature battle field. Rifles, great coats, helmets, dead and wounded horses and men, not many of the latter thank God but a lot of the former strewed the ground while the trampled and bloodstained grass told its own tale. At first sight, from where I stood I counted 10 dead horses without searching. How men escaped is a miracle for which we thank God, but we had only one killed and three wounded, one (the one I mentioned, Jim Thomson of Canterbury Squadron severely). One of my mates had a bullet put slap through the crown of his hat.

Those hit were carted back to camp and the available Mtd troops chased the Jackies until dinner time. How many horses were wounded is not exactly known. The Boers captured a lot and we had about 15 or sixteen killed in action. The Boers captured mine and my saddle and bridle and I'm now dismounted but I got away with my overcoat rifle and ammunition so must be thankful.

The Boers were very plucky and in that light behaved splendidly and so did our fellows when the first scare was over. The fog made good shooting impossible or many more would have been hit as the Boers and our fellows were that close that they were shouting to each other and calling each other such names as will not bear repetition here. The Boers did a very clever thing and sneaked right on to us in the fog coming so close that they were mistaken by Col Garratt himself for our own Scouts when they were spotted. They fired into the mass of men and horses from 15 to 20 yards so you can fancy how things were with us. For us to reply at once was impossible, we were too much packed up so we just made off to cover. My word the Officers revolvers were whipped out in quick time that morning but it is over.

January 1902

Some of the battles between the opposing sides were bitter, hard-fought hand-to-hand affairs, as shown in this artist's depiction. (Courtesy Hocken Library, Dunedin)

Soldier Boy

It was an experience and a lesson which, all things considered, Thank God, was very cheaply bought. Two mornings ago we had another New Zealander shot through the chest and spine, and he is dying now. Poor fellow it's a sad New Year for him. Three of the Hussars were captured too.

The Boers are very numerous and "willing" out this way but we must not be dismayed. There is a convoy coming in now so I will stop as there might be a mail for us on it and if there is I will be able to answer it in this so Ta Ta. I forgot to tell you that three or four days after Xmas we each got a parcel from Natal and it was very thankfully received. It was very thoughtful of them wasn't it.

Au Revoir

Later in the evening

There was no mail for us on the convoy though we hear that there will be one coming out in the course of a few days. Of course we must take this for what it's worth as we have been listening to that story ever since we left Bothas Fort. I suppose it will come some day and no doubt when it does put in an appearance it will come in force. We hope so at "anyhow" as Barrie used to say.

I have a little to tell you now which might please you. It is this. After all there is not going to be many stay here and join the 8th if they can help it, so I have made up my mind that unless it is compulsory to stay I will leave this country as soon as my time is up. As far as war goes the Boers are beaten and badly beaten long ago and I am perfectly willing to let those who have a liking for the game we have been playing this last eight months finish it. I have had quite enough Active Service to give me an insight into the way of war and I will count myself as one of the specially favoured ones if I get out of it with a whole skin. I am going a long way ahead I know but God has spared me thus far and I trust him to see me through.

If we have to stay here it's a different thing and I shall be perfectly willing to be where the Regiment is. I believe that twelve weeks from now will see us off the treck and practically done with night alarms as I hear that we mobilise at the beginning of April. I can't help but hope that it is so. You will see by the papers however before that time. One thing I must say. Don't be too eager to see me back because a deuce of a lot of bullets can be fired in three months and not that alone. I have a very pressing invitation to go to England when I am done here and after this country's hot Summer it would suit me fine to miss the NZ winter and get back about September. However I know nothing yet. We may not be able to obtain leave to do that and if we can there is the question of finance to be considered but to be plain with you I must say I am greatly in favour with seeing the Coronation if I can.

Just another thing. When you see reports in the paper about us going to embark for home don't absolutely stop your supply of letters. They are bound to appear about a dozen times before we really start and I'm sure you'd sooner have a few letters returned to you than have me going without a mail for so long. But don't write after March 31st unless you see that we are going to stay on.

Whips of love from
Harry

Soldier Boy

For Dad

Iaddress these letters to mother because if I sent them to yourself you might be away when they arrive and I am conceited enough to think that the people at home like to open my letters as soon as they arrive which they could not do if they were for you and you were away at the time they came. So you must not think there is any slight implied.

Your aff son
Harry

Orange River Colony, Haaihoek
January 29th 1902

Dear Father, Mother and All

It's a good time since I wrote my last letter and I am going to try and make a start with another though it must be short this time as I am just about out of paper and have only one envelope to my name.

It's seven weeks ago since we left the Railway and we have no money and you may say no nothing. I don't know when this will be posted for there is no word about a mail either coming or going. It's a month now since I had my last from you or nearly so but I expect there is mail waiting for us somewhere. I had a letter from Jessie, written in Darfield, something over a fortnight ago and by the same mail I got a couple of *Evening Stars* telling about the earthquakes in New Zealand.

They appear to have been pretty severe but this will be an old story by the time this reaches you. You must excuse pencil and scribble this time as I am in a deuce of a hurry and have to get this done as soon as possible.

Since writing my last we have been in the thick of the Boers as per usual. This district is the busiest in the whole of the War now. We are no longer at blockhouse work, we have been off that for a fortnight now. The Jackies are very thick about here and are full of fight.

The morning before we left the blockhouse work they got on to a patrol of Hussars who were with us at the time and a hard fight resulted. The Hussars made a splendid stand but were outnumbered. However they held their position until we could get out to assist them with the guns. They had 5 killed 9 wounded and 13 captured. The Boers also lost a good many men but as they had it all in their own hands they got their dead and those who were hit away with the exception of one dead man who was killed as they finally retired. They charged at the Hussars repeatedly and in the bravest fashion and carried their wounded out of the fire in the pluckiest style. However they shot one Hussar in cold Blood and buried him. The other four we took into camp and buried that night. It was a sad business.

They attacked us after we left the blockhouse but another lot of troops came up with a Colt gun and a pom pom and Mr Jackie had to get.

This last week we have been operating in conjunction with two other columns

Soldier Boy

under Col Bing and Dunlop. Their Mounted force is composed of South African Light Horse, Imp Yeomanry and Royal Artillery Mtd Rifles. We have been moving about with about 2500 Mtd men 6 big guns 2 pom poms a Colt and a Maxim and some have been having plenty of fight.

On Saturday the Boers rushed a pom pom under the SALH but were beaten off, it was a dead willing go and worth seeing. Their gun went out of action full gallop and ours came up at the same pace and opened at top. Some of the Light Horse have been killed and some wounded. Our gun got the range onto some Boers and sent three shells into them and over went one and his horse smash. They were beaten off but they were very plucky in fact you could truthfully say rash.

I don't know just how many prisoners we took but it was a few. One was dressed in our uniform and the law now is that such men be tried as spies and shot. He was Court Martialled, sentenced and shot the next day at noon just before camp shifted.

It seems a cruel thing to stand a man up beside his own grave and shoot him but it's just enough, for a man in our uniform is simply a murderer in the fighting. I don't want to see another man so treated though, for it's a sickener marching a man up to an open grave with his eyes open.

As he marched up and saw the grave he asked if there was no mercy but a sorrowful shake of the head from the Sergt of the firing party was the only answer. He asked again when his eyes were bandaged but got the same reply and clasping his hands in prayer he stood up and died like a man. I'll never forget the silence the crack of the volley and then the silence again. It would give anyone the creeps.

I don't think our Colonel would have shot him for being in khaki alone, but it was proved that he got the uniform off a wounded officer whom he killed with a pick in the cruelest fashion.

I hope we won't see the same again. Shooting a man in action is not so bad but to stand one up blindfolded and his hands tied behind him and level the rifles on him is a different thing. There was no colonials in the firing party thank goodness or some of us might have funked it.

I must stop now and leave writing for some more favourable opportunity.

Heaps of Love from
Harry

SA, Heilbron, ORC
February 10th 1902

It's over a week since I wrote my last and it has not been posted yet. You will think that you are all completely forgotten this time but I really can't help it this time as we have been after the Jackies and have had no time to do or think of anything else. I'm very sorry though because I know you will be looking for a letter.

We got into here last night and are keeping a standing camp today and drawing Remounts. I got a letter from you last night and a couple of Outlooks. Your letter had a sheet from Lottie in it and a slip from Dad.

We have been having another tough time and have been on short rations again but I must not burden your time with accounts of that. We have been doing a lot of fighting too but I won't go into a lengthy description of that either.

One thing I must tell you although you will see it in the papers before this reaches you is that we (the 7th) have had the honour to capture De Wets guns in fair fight. 2 Pom Poms 1 Fifteen pounder and 1 ammunition wagon. Of this bit or work we are proud, and pardonably so and we have been complimented by our Colonels and by Lord Kitchener himself who calls it a bit of Smart and Gallant work.

You peaceable people at home will of course see nothing to be proud of in this and will take no pride in it but we out here who know what guns are feel very different about it when we know that it was ourselves who had to do the bustling for them. I'm not going to start skiting about how we did it but it was close going for awhile. We had two killed and one wounded. We killed three Boers wounded some more (one of whom died soon afterwards on our wagons) and captured 15 I think it was.

Of course all the Contingent wasn't there only a few of us but it was New Zealanders alone who did it and as I said before we are proud. A funny thing is that one of the Pom Poms is the very one which shelled us same fellows on June 25th of last year and nearly put my lights out for one. That was out from Greylingstadt at Watervaalhoek.

We have been taking part in a big move out here this last week and have captured a deuce of a lot of Boers. But you will see all about this in the papers.

You must excuse the scribble as I am writing this in a very different position to that in which yours are done. I can't answer Lottie's or Dad's this time. I'm clean out of money paper and every flaming thing but if I'm spared I'll be able to tell you all the news in a few months time and if not, well we've captured some guns anyway.

I hope you are all well. Walt Jones and Steve W are well. F Chambers (the Baker) was supposed to be dying of enteric last night and I don't know how he is this morning.

Goodbye for this time.

Love to all
From
Harry

Orange Free State, Albertina, near Harrismith
28ʰ February 1902

Dear Father Mother and All

I have had no letters from any of you since writing my last from Heilbron but as we are halting at this siding and expecting a mail this afternoon I am going to try and scribble a few lines to let you know how things are with us.

Well we have been having a deuce of a hard time again one way and another since we started our last treck out. I may as well come at the worst at once and tell you about the reverse we got from the Boers the other night. But I shouldn't call it a reverse for the Jackies got the worst of it by far but the price paid by us was a dear one.

Long before you get this you will have been shocked to see that in one short fight the New Zealand 7ᵗʰ lost over sixty killed and wounded and you will no doubt have passed through a period of great anxiety waiting for particulars and names of those whose fate it was to go down. What I have to say about it will be stale news to you but coming from the spot you may think it worth the reading.

Well since the lines of blockhouses have been completed we have been working things a different way to what we used to. Instead of one column moving about by itself they move from six to a dozen together and they keep touch with each other on either flank. Thus a tremendous stretch of front is covered and everything is swept before the advancing troops until a line of blockhouses is reached when Mr Jackie has either to put up a fight or else surrender. The Boers have not much chance of getting through the blockhouses and their only chance of getting through the troops is at night as you will see.

To prevent this the country is lined across for miles every night with outposts every 60 or 70 yards apart and about six men on a post. On the night of the disaster this is what our troops were at. I may mention here that I was not on duty that night only being discharged from the Field hospital that day where I had been down with an attack of Malaria. I was bad with that at Heilbron but I didn't say anything about it as I expected to be soon better however it was not so as I got worse and went to the mischief for a while but that's neither here nor there. I'm not in hospital now.

Well on the night of the 23rd the Boers in force attacked the posts of our left wing (composed of Canterbury, Otago and Supplementary Coys 24, 25, 26). Over a thousand of the enemy were engaged and in an hour all the men on the posts were either dead or wounded with the exception of a few who were captured or escaped. Of the Canterbury boys 40 odd went out and only 10 came back all the rest being knocked over 10 killed and the rest more or less badly wounded. Cant Coy had just about half of the total number of casualties so you can see they were in the thickest of it.

Not being in it I am not going to describe the fight though I know only too well what it was like. Spencer was in it and he was one of the lucky ones who escaped unhit. I was in bed when the fighting started but being so used to hearing the like took no notice and was soon asleep.

The Boers fought in splendid style advancing without fear and as fast as their men fell they were picked up and put on horses by Kaffirs who were with them. They just advanced along the line of trenches from one post to another and mowed our men down with a fire that must have been hell itself. Of course nothing could stop them and they got through as they intended. Next morning over sixty of our brave fellows were lying on the ground.

I won't sicken you by describing this part of the business but every trench had its little black heap of dead and wounded and the groaning was heartrending to hear I believe. Our Regimental Colonel Porter was cut up just as if they had all been his own sons, and even Hardened old Col White, when he went up and saw the long line of dead and wounded, could scarcely speak. For a few minutes he looked on in silence his eyes moist and his face twitching suspiciously then turning around he said "Look at them how they lie. Every man down in his own trench. See what a stand they have made. Soldiers and men every inch of them," and with his own hands he helped to fix the wounded.

In spite of their pluck the Boers had not been able to get all their men who were hit away. Their wounded were attended to and their dead (27) were buried in one grave by our chaps. I helped in the hospital with our wounded when they came in and it was horrible. One died on the way in and he had to be buried at once and I had to lend a hand with that. May I never be mixed up in the same again. Not that I object to helping the wounded but I hope that there will never again be the necessity for it.

I must leave this now, more later if possible.

Later . . .

Here's for another try. I had to stop as Lord Kitchener and his staff arrived to have a look at the camp, and us fellows. He's a great boy is Kitchener there's no humbug about him. He didn't cause as much flutter in the lines as a usual rifle inspection does. He praised the New Zealanders up and said in his straight plain way that he was glad the Boers got on to us that night as "it would teach them a lesson." This from him is something.

Then he said "I suppose you're a bit tired boys." He got a quick "Yes sir," I promise you. "Oh well," he says with a grim sort of smile "Never mind, you'll be at it again in a day or two."

He told us how many Boers were captured this move (over 600) and also that he had this morning seen and had a word with all our wounded in Harrismith hospital and sent a cable of condolence to the Premier of NZ for the parents and relatives of those killed. There was no gush about him at all just straight from the shoulder.

The descriptions you read of him are pretty near the mark. In life he is much the same to look at as in a picture only the scowl is less pronounced but I wouldn't like to have him onto my brass for anything.

Regarding the number of Boers placed hors de combat in the fight the other night our fellows sold their lives very dearly as besides the 27 buried by us and the few wounded taken, Remingtons column on our left came across 96 wounded Jackies in a Boer hospital. He took 16 away but the rest were too bad to bother with as prisoners so he left them. How many they had already buried goodness knows. Still that won't bring back the dead.

Some of us can't help thinking of the sad hearts there are in NZ today. Mothers, Sisters, and Sweethearts, who have had the short and cruel cable of "killed" come to them from over the sea where some dear one has been struck down by the hand of fate. Many a tear will be shed at the thought of the lonely grave which they can never see or tend and how often will the vain regret "If I could only of seen him die" be uttered by those who are left to mourn.

If they only knew the look of the reality out here they would thank God that they did not see, for one glance would be enough to haunt them all their days. To them Death at any rate will suggest folded hands and peaceful faces and it is best so, but many a heart in NZ will be buried in that one grave where 22 of our late comrades are sleeping. There is no more hunger or night alarms, no more wet bivouacs under a pelting rain for them their trecking is done and they are at rest. Who knows, but what those of us who are left behind are the worst off. Bert Turner was shot dead and he lay there with a smile on his face as if death had no fears for him. They are gone and we have to go on with the treck until our time comes or our term of service is past, but we need not fret our fate is in higher hands than ours and the Boers don't always get their own way.

I must leave this for tonight now. I hear a mail has arrived so perhaps tomorrow I may have a letter from you to answer. I hope so anyhow so, Adieu.

Saturday Morning March 1ˢᵗ

There was a mail arrived all right and I got letters from Joe and Fred Louis Mother and Jessie so I did not do so bad. As I must try and answer all of these today I must ask you to excuse me if I do not put much more to this.

We hear that the NZ 8th landed at Durban yesterday and that 100 are coming up the line to join us. I don't know whether this is true or not. I pity the poor beggars who join us if it is so as they will have a rough time of it for a start. This last treck we were four days without even an issue of biscuits and talk about hunger. Jerusalem. I missed a part of the rough time as I was in hospital getting port wine and tinned roast fowl but to say that I noticed the change when I came out still pretty shaky gives no idea of how I really got on.

The other night we did not camp until late and it was raining and my mate and I, being tired,

Soldier Boy

turned in under a wagon without even lighting a fire. We had not a bite of food with us and it was dismal. At last after a lengthy search we got three spoonfuls of dry oatmeal and we ate that but we went hungry to sleep I can tell you. Such is life out here.

I must get on with my other letters now so hoping you are all well. Believe me.

Your As Ever
H G Gilbert

On a separate sheet of paper Harry wrote a detailed list of casualties from the battle which took place on February 23rd, referred to in the above letter. It is believed he included this separate list in with the general letter home, but wrote it specifically for his father.

Dear Father

This list shows only the losses in my own Squadron. Over as many more were hit in the other two Companies of our Left Wing including 12 (I think) killed. Canterbury Company lost all its Officers and Sergeants and was completely smashed up so to speak. Those of my Company who were out that night and escaped unhit were Corpls Spencer, Kane, Foster, Hardie, Cooper. Troopers McKenzie D McKenzie J Waters, Tomlinson, Creemer, out of 42.

When you notice how many were hit by two or more bullets you will be able to form some slight idea of what the firing was like; one man in the Otago Coy has five through him. Westropp the artist friend of mine who I told you about as first meeting at Glentui was shot through the foot and hips but is doing well.

Canterbury Casualties

Bushman's Drift

February 23rd 1902

Killed:
Captain Dickenson (Christchurch)
Lieutenant Forsyth (Auckland)
Sergeant Noonan (Akaroa)
Corporal. Boddick (Temuka)
Trooper Whitney (Timaru)
Trooper Counahan (Waimate)
Trooper Stevenson (Timaru)
Trooper Bruce (Ashburton)
Trooper Monahan (Temuka)
Trooper Tims (Christchurch)

Wounded:

Trooper + McKlellan	4
Trooper + Dunford	2
Trooper + McDermid	2
Trooper Isbister	2
+ Trooper Cook W	1
Trooper Reynolds	1
Farrier Ross	3
Trooper Kelley	1
+Lieutenant Colledge	1
Lieutenant Wilson	1
Sergeant Malcolm	1
Sergeant Langford	1
Sergeant Minife	1
Corporal Scott	1
Corporal Westropp	2
+*Corporal Rosanoski	2
Trooper Frame	1
Trooper Boon	
Trooper Rodgers	2
Trooper Hardie	2
+Trooper Ditely	3
Corpl Legg	2

+ Seriously wounded

* Has had left arm amputated

Figures opposite names of wounded denote number of bullets they were struck by

Farrier Bert Turner of Amberley (Killed) though a Canterbury boy had been attached to the Sup (26) Coy ever since leaving the boat

Lieutenant Forsyth (Killed) was a native of Auckland but he belonged to the Canterbury (24) Squadron and my (No. 2) troop.

Soldier Boy

Amelia 750 ORC, South Africa, near Botha's Pass
April 6th 1902

Dear Mother, Father and All

Just a few hurried lines in answer to a big mail which reached me yesterday. I will have to make it short and sweet this time as we have very little time for writing and I have to send a letter to Joe this time. I'm very sorry but I can't get time to answer Lottie's long letter which came to hand with the rest you will have to make this one go round all hands. I must not try and go into my doing since writing last or I will have to stop long before I am finished. We got into here yesterday and are off again I believe early in the morning so you will see how things are.

I am well and doing alright and so are most of the boys though we have been having a very rough time of it lately. We were joined here by 130 details which came over with the 8th Canty to reinforce us. They are a fine clean looking lot compared to our fellows but they will lose all that when they get fairly going on the veldt.

We have not got much longer to do now about a fortnight's trecking and driving I think so by the time you get this we will be off the Veldt and preparing for home if we don't stop a bullet between then and now and none of us want to do that. I hear the 8th Canty itself is in Newcastle but would not be sure about it.

I got the photo of Mother (Grannie) and the wee Harry in your letters yesterday. How like that little photo you have of me he is, or at least it seems to me to be so. I also had news from England yesterday as well as a long letter from Joe. All the Christmas presents which were sent from NZ for us only got up to us last night. Rather late for Christmas but acceptable still. Some of the Cake and stuff was rotten but much was good and today we are living off tinned fish and fruit, potted meats, jam and plum puddings beside having a good supply of cigarettes and tobacco. It's either a feast or a famine out here and before many more weeks are past if we are still on the veldt we will be longing for more of the stuff we are now eating to waste.

I can't say whether I will get to England or not yet but will let you know later if possible. Sorry I can't write more now but can't help it. Heaps of love

From
Harry

South Africa, Newcastle, Natal
April 12th 1902

My Dear Father

I received your very welcome letter on April 5th but as I explained in a short letter to Mother I had no chance to answer it then. However I have the chance now and am going to try and scribble you a few lines though how many I would not like to say for although I have comparatively plenty of time on my hand still there is a tendency to lie low and take a good spell when it is offered which up to date has been very seldom.

You will see by Mother's how it is that I am here so I need not go into it again but rather let you have some short account of how our last few months on the treck have been spent. It has been harder lately than ever it was before, with us at

any rate and we haven't had the easiest times right from the very start.

These drives are going to finish the war but they will have their effect on our troops as well as those of Mr Jackie, if such men can be called troops which they can't.

I have not written home since we were at Harrismith until the other day so if I give you an account of our doings since leaving there it won't be stale news to you.

I told you about our smash up and sent a list of casualties so I need not mention this again.

Well when we left that place our columns straightway lined up for another drive toward the Pretoria–Cape line this time. All went well until we got near to Heilbron and then Boers started to show themselves and prisoners began to come in. One night orders came out that "Troops will march 31 miles tomorrow. One day's rations for men and horses to be carried on horse. Convoy will be left behind and no kits carried." Next morning at daybreak we were off with nothing but our overcoats. The country was bad and as per usual the day was roasting hot but on we had to go. We could not travel fast and it was settling down for dark when we drew into camp. We had no dinner that day and little to drink so you can imagine how we felt after riding that distance.

But just as we were lined up along comes orders "Boers reported on the right front. Outpost to go out at once". Here was a go. No blankets, no tea and tired bones and Boers in front. Out we had to go. It was now night and we were so done that we didn't dig a trench but got extended and laid down in the grass to sleep.

About ten o'clock the Picket Officer came along and wanted to know why we were not entrenched. We told him we had no tools and were too tired anyhow. "Oh," he says, "it's no good. It's an army order that all outposts must be entrenched I'll get a spade for you." So he did and the whole post had to turn out and start to work in the dark. When my turn came I just dug a hole for myself and turned into it.

What sort of a cold and hungry night I put in I will leave you to imagine but we were all glad when daylight put in an appearance. Then we were off again with just a bite for breakfast. That night the wagons could not get up with us so once again we had to sleep out without blankets.

My post was in some old ruined Kaffir Kraals that night and it was just one swarming nest of mosquitoes until the cold got the better of them. We laid down and got to sleep when the firing started. We made sure the Boers were on us and we got into action quick. Whizz goes the bullets and plunk goes one into our wall. It was lively but it was only an old sniper or two and was soon over.

When next morning came we did not feel particularly refreshed but we had to be off again, this time into the railway at Vredefort Road. We were all certain of a spell there but at daybreak we had to move down the line to Lieuw Spruit to reinforce the blockhouses on the line. Squadrons had to keep saddled up all night ready to move off at five minutes, notice and in the daytime likewise while us fellows had to sleep in full rig which is not too comfortable.

Two o'clock next afternoon we suddenly got word to move back to Vredefort Road. This we did and each one was saying to his mate "We're sure to get a spell this time". Imagine our feelings when on being lined up word comes to "Offsaddle until 7 tonight. At that time all Mounted troops and Artillery will move out in a night march. Rations to be carried. Convoy will follow at 3AM tomorrow." Of that nights march I will say nothing but sleep and spills were the order of the day (or night). Next morning at daybreak we surrounded and rushed the town of Parijs (Paris) but found the Boers gone.

We trecked about there for three or four days and then put back into Vredefort Road. But even this time there was no rest for us for after loading the convoy we started onto the veldt again on the drive I have just come off.

On that move we were blocked by the Wilge River for nearly a week and had to cross it at last while it was rolling down like an ocean. About 50 mules were drowned and two men also. How many wagons were lost I don't know but I do know that we got a ducking both with rain and river. A few nights after that the Boers or some of them broke through our lines. There was another stiff fight, we had two killed and some wounded (of the Munster Fusiliers). At last we got to Botha's Pass and from there I and the rest of the dismounted came on to here and if we are laying on our oars and inclined to be lazy I am sure you will look over it and think of what we have so lately been going through.

As I told Mother we are trying to have a good easy time and so far have succeeded not too badly. Our officers say that we have done with the veldt and though this sounds too good to be true we all hope most sincerely that it is so.

Our Colonel is at present in Pretoria. We had a wire from him this morning saying that some men from the 6th 7th 8th and 9th Contingents were to be sent home under him for the Coronation. I won't be amongst these I don't expect as my

Soldier Boy

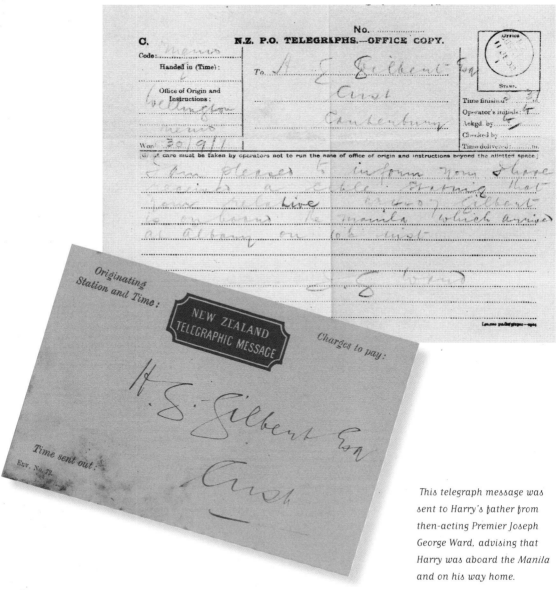

This telegraph message was sent to Harry's father from then-acting Premier Joseph George Ward, advising that Harry was aboard the Manila *and on his way home.*

application is apart from this and I won't be tall enough either as they say 5ft 10 is the height required and I can't quite reach that.

But I don't fret if I don't get home on my own. I'll have far more liberty than I would do if I went with a Contingent. But of this I can say nothing definite. I will write from Cape Town if possible but if I don't don't expect me home when the 7th arrives as you might get a disappointment. I will certainly go to the old country if I can get leave and finance will allow but as yet I do not know.

I was very pleased to get your letter to hear you were all so well and busy. If I stay away much longer you will be forgetting that you ever had me home. But that's only the way of the world and is especially noticeable out here. However "We're Sons of the Empire and we're ready when they pipe all hands". As the song says we are "Fighting for the dear old colours, Marching on to war, With the hearts we love behind us and the Flag we love before." So let it be until such times as wars cease. Someone must do the fighting for those who cause it won't that's certain.

Excuse my hurried caligraphy and such blunders as may have occurred in my grammar. Hope to see you before I face another shell.

As Ever Your Aff Son
HG Gilbert Jnr

Soldier Boy

These New Zealand returned troopers parade back in their own land after their year of service in South Africa. (Courtesy Hocken Library, Dunedin)

The Camp, Horoeka
September 6ᵗʰ 1902

Dear Mother and All

Once again from a bush camp I am I am going to write to you. I don't know whether it seems strange for you to get a letter from me at this place but I can say it seems terribly strange for me to be back here again. Up at the old whare things are so much changed that it does not seem quite like what it used to be, but down here in a bush camp it seems like a slice out of the days that are past. As I was saying to Joe just now, it seems like a dream that I have got back at all. The old flapping galley, waving trees, the moreporks and the smell of rata smoke is just like what it used to be.

It was raining when I left Wellington on Thursday morning but it cleared off as we got up into the Wairarapa. I went straight on into Makuri that night and next morning it was raining again in fine style. I suppose it had followed us up in the meantime.

You will see I am not beating round the bush now as regards work but am getting straight off the mark seeing that I only arrived here yesterday and have been working all day today. That's not so bad is it – but of course my holiday is over now until next time.

You may not believe it but good old Glen knew me again after nearly three years away, so truly the hand that floggeth them they know. He is developing into a good old has been and just as fat as butter and too lazy for most things. It's rather surprising after Canterbury to come up here and see the quantity of feed they have for this time of year.

I must stop now and "Umba lala" as the Kaffirs say, but I am done with time now for a while anyhow. Remember me to all the people who may enquire and give my love to Mrs Cromie. Don't get working too hard at your spring outfits and think sometimes of your nuisance that's departed and believe him still to be.

Yours as ever
HG Gilbert

This abridged letter appears to be Harry's first letter to his family after his return to New Zealand and follows a holiday at home with them in Cust. After the holiday he then apparently went back to his uncle's farm at Horoeka, east of Pahiatua.

Soldier Boy

This hut at Horoeka was home for Harry during his years as a scrub-cutter before he went to war in 1899 and it was where he returned a little more than a year later. (GILBERT FAMILY COLLECTION)

Harry Gilbert's Certificate of Discharge, dated 15th September, 1902, showing that he had served 1 year and 87 days as a trooper.

Present Day

E lsa Wood, in early 2007 aged 85, is the third of four children by Harry Gilbert
and his wife Florence, and was born in the Presbyterian manse in Invercargill.
She has a good and detailed memory of her childhood and of both her parents, but
says that her father rarely if ever spoke of his own childhood, or of his family, or of
his time as a soldier in the Boer War.

He was, she says, a man of strong principles and somewhat Victorian in his
manner and way of life. A state of extreme casual dress for him – such as when
on holiday at the family bach at Raglan during the summer – was long woollen
trousers, a white shirt and a waistcoat. However, his tie may have been a little
loosened at the neck. At almost all other times he was to be seen in a three-piece
suit with closely knotted tie, Fedora hat, and, in the winter, a calf-length black
heavy woollen coat.

When Harry Gilbert came back to New Zealand from the Boer War, it seems
that he did not come back via Great Britain (or "home" as he referred to it several
times in his letters) as he had hinted at in several of his later letters from South
Africa. Rather, he must have come home directly on a troop ship. That must have
got him back to his family in Cust about June or July 2002, because after some
time with them he travelled north to Wellington and then on up through the
Wairarapa, finally making his way back out to the scrub-cutting camp he had left
less than 18 months previously, at Horoeka, east of Pahiatua.

In August 1902 Harry received from the Commandant of the New Zealand
Defence Forces an Imperial South African War medal for service in South Africa
and also clasps for service in Transvaal and Orange Free State.

His official Certificate of Discharge from the army is dated September 15th,
1902, and shows that Harry served one year and 87 days abroad. It also shows he
was paid a war gratuity for his service.

Interestingly, this is one of the few documents which refers to the war as the
"2nd Boer war". Many New Zealanders are unaware that a decade earlier (1889–91)
there was an earlier war fought between British and Boer soldiers in South Africa,
in which the British were soundly beaten.

How long Harry continued to work as a scrub-cutter at Horoeka on his return
to New Zealand is not known, but we know he spent some time during 1906 in

Harry saw service again when World War 1 broke out some 13 years after his return from the Boer War. This time he went to war as Captain Reverend Harry Gilbert, military chaplain 4ᵗʰ class, with the New Zealand Expeditionary Force. (GILBERT FAMILY COLLECTION)

Soldier Boy

England. Soon after Harry came home, possibly in 1906, he underwent training as a Presbyterian minister at Knox College in Dunedin.

On December 22nd, 1914, Harry married Florence Margaret Carrington in Dunedin. Subsequently, Harry was posted to a Presbyterian church at Maheno, just south of Oamaru, where their first son, Harold, was born. By mid-June 1916, the presbytery at Oamaru (which must have also been in charge of the Maheno church) was considering the need for chaplains to be appointed to the New Zealand Territorial Forces being sent to Europe as part of the Allied forces involved in World War 1.

A minuted note from a special meeting of the presbytery, dated June 15th, 1916, states that the presbytery "unanimously recommends to the Defence Department the appointment of the Rev Henry George Gilbert as a Territorial Chaplain with a view to his subsequently going to the Front with the Expeditionary Forces.

"Mr Gilbert was a member of the 7th N.Z. Contingent in the South African War and has had a good deal of military experience in this country, and we believe him to be eminently fitted for the duties of Chaplain."

Four days later, the minuted note was despatched with an accompanying letter to the Hon J Allen, MP, Minister of Defence, Wellington, commending Rev Gilbert to an appointment in the Territorial Forces.

Harry was accepted by the army, and joined the 2nd Battalion Otago Regiment as a Chaplain 4th class, with the rank of Captain and regimental number 50,000 in July 1916. His record for World War 1 shows he went into Camp Featherston, north of Wellington, almost immediately. His wife must have accompanied him, because their second child, Ruth, was born in Camp Featherston in March 1917. Within a month of her birth, Harry sailed (on 26th April, 1917) in the Turakina to Devonport in Auckland, where he was "taken on strength with seniority" with the New Zealand Expeditionary Force.

On February 26th, 1918 he was ordered to join the NZEF in France. The record of his service in Europe is scant, but shows that he returned to London in June 1919, and finally sailed for New Zealand aboard the Corinthic on August 9th, 1919.

When he returned home, Harry took up his duties as a Presbyterian minister, and was again posted to St Paul's Presbyterian church in Invercargill, where his last two children were born – Else in 1922, and Len in 1924.

In 1925 the family moved to St Andrew's church in Hamilton, and his daughter recalls that he and his wife "loaded all us four kids and all their belongings into his car, a big Chevrolet, and in spite of the rough roads in those days he drove all the way from Invercargill to Hamilton. That car was the first all-glassed-in car the people of Hamilton had ever seen."

After several years in Hamilton, he bought a holiday property at Raglan, on the west coast of the North Island. The property included a tiny bach set in seven acres of pine and native bush forest, and from then on the Gilbert family would spend every possible opportunity at their bach.

"There was no one else around there, and we had wonderful times there, playing on the beach and in the bush," says Elsa Wood. "My father had a tiny workshop there, and he spent hours in there with his wood and his tools."

As he grew older, Harry Gilbert worked more and more with wood, in the process teaching himself to make violins. Members of the family were always very careful when they opened a cupboard because they were more likely to find violin pieces hanging from rails or hooks.

"He was always experimenting with woods and varnishes", recalls Mrs Wood We'd often see the violin skeletons hanging in the wardrobes, drying, and we weren't allowed to go anywhere near them. The days that we always laughed about were when he was bending the ribs of the violin. He would have a pot of water on the gas ring, and inside the pot was the glue-pot with the glue softening. Then Dad would start bending the ribs across a piece of iron, and if one of them broke he would be extremely angry, and we would stay out of the kitchen for the day.

He made about a dozen violins over the years, cutting out the delicate pieces, fitting and gluing them together and then finishing them with his own specially brewed varnish. Several of these violins are still owned by family members.

Harry stayed on the army's reserves list as a chaplain for some years, finally retiring from that list in February 1948, two years after he had retired from the ministry and his position at St Andrew's in Hamilton.

His wife Florence died in 1942 after a prolonged illness, and when he retired from the ministry Harry moved into a compact house on the eastern end of Beale Street in Hamilton East, within walking distance of St Andrew's Church.

He died there on November 11th, 1954, at the age of 73, after suffering a massive heart attack.

First published in 2007 by
New Holland Publishers (NZ) Ltd
Auckland • Sydney • London • Cape Town

www.newhollandpublishers.co.nz

218 Lake Road, Northcote, Auckland, New Zealand
Unit 1, 66 Gibbes Street, Chatswood, NSW 2067, Australia
86–88 Edgware Road, London W2 2EA, United Kingdom
80 McKenzie Street, Cape Town 8001, South Africa

Conceived and packaged for New Holland Publishers
in 2007 by Renaissance Publishing,
PO Box 36 206, Northcote, Auckland

Design: Trevor Newman
Editor: Renée Lang

A catalogue record for this book is available from
the National Library of New Zealand

ISBN: 978 1 86966 177 9

Printed in China by SNP Leefung

10 9 8 7 6 5 4 3 2 1

Front cover: Trooper Harry Gilbert before setting off for South Africa in April 1901 with the 7th Canterbury Mounted Rifles. (Gilbert Family Collection)